Spiritual Practices

THE
SACRED
WAY

for Everyday Life

BY TONY JONES

ZONDERVAN™

GRAND RAPIDS, MICHIGAN 49530 USA

Sacred Way
Copyright © 2004 by Youth Specialties

Youth Specialties Books, 300 South Pierce Street, El Cajon, CA 92020, are published by
Zondervan, 5300 Patterson Avenue SE, Grand Rapids, MI 49530

Library of Congress Cataloging-in-Publication Data
Jones, Tony, 1968-
 The sacred way : spiritual practices for everyday life / by Tony Jones.
   p. cm.
 Includes bibliographical references (p. 203-224).
 ISBN 0-310-25810-3 (pbk.)
 1. Spiritual life--Christianity. I. Title.
 BV4501.3.J663 2005
 248.4'6--dc22

                                                                    2004023720

Editorial direction by Carla Barnhill
Art direction by Jay Howver
Proofreading by Laura Gross
Cover design by Rule 29
Interior design by David Conn
Cover photo by Greg Gerla/luckyPix/Veer
Author photo by Thom Olson

Printed in the United States of America

---

04 05 06 07 / DC / 10 9 8 7 6 5 4 3 2 1

DEDICATED TO

Aidan McMahon Jones

Welcome to God's World

table of contents

foreword

Thomas Wolfe once famously observed that we can never go home again. He was, and still is, correct, of course. We can't. But because we can never go home again, we human beings have learned to compensate for our loss or, more correctly put, we have learned to turn it to our progress as individuals and as a species. We have learned to carry the best of home away with us. While in our youth we may energetically push aside all the dreadful and the compromising things that have been home, in our maturity we tend to turn back across the years and reclaim at least some of the tools and objects, principles and treasures that informed and shaped us while we were still there. We reclaim them; and then we teach ourselves to make from them new homes and new souls who are both the same as, and different from, that out of which we came. That same progress from separation through reclamation to renewal and revitalization is very much in process right now in American Christianity, most especially in American Protestant Christianity.

Once was the time when Christianity was more of a piece than it is now. Once was the time, in the centuries before the Great Schism separated East from West and before the Reformation severed Protestant from Roman Catholic. Once was the time in those precedent centuries when the disciplines of devotion and religious formation were the understood and almost routine rhythms of daily Christian life in the world. They were the ways of home for the Christian spirit. But West broke with East and, in time, protesting and confessing church broke with parent church; and for the protestors in particular, what had been home no longer could be.

Like most youthful innocents, we Protestants first set our course by denying all those tools and objects, principles and treasures that had informed and shaped us. Indeed, we threw them aside quite violently and with monumental contempt, judging them to be not only worthless but, far worse, to be the proofs and evidences of a benighted and dangerously less grace-filled time. Now, five centuries later, we begin to understand, as do all maturing creatures who are granted a sufficiency of years, that the good in us was not entirely all of our own making. In fact, we begin to suspect that in our forebears there lay some dear wisdom as well as much dank error, that in our common beginnings there were some truths and some habits of formation that nourished them and whose loss has diminished us. But if, indeed, we can not go home again—if indeed we are very clear about the fact that we positively do not wish to go home again—how do we address this aching sense of loss, of incompleteness, of half-remembered engagement with the shaping of our souls? It is a good question. In fact, it is, I suspect, THE question for more and more Protestants today.

* * * * *

Tony Jones is a leader of, and major force within, what is being called the emerging Church, or the emergent Church or, more simply, the new or re-forming Christianity. For several years in his role as a Protestant youth minister, Jones learned to read carefully and pastor well the hearts and souls of a rising generation of American Protestants who increasingly yearned for the church of the proto-fathers and mothers of their faith; who yearned for the passion and clarity that were the church of the first century; who wanted to go, not home, but to what Robert Webber calls "the ancient-future." Now as an academic and doctoral candidate at Princeton Theological Seminary,

Jones spends himself by shifting through the intervening and obfuscating centuries to ferret out those treasures of the early church's practices that formed the first of us and that, pray God, will form the ancient future that more and more of us long to call home. This book is a kind of first-fruits of all of those years and both those roles.

❈ ❈ ❈ ❈ ❈

This is a sturdy book. In all my years of talking about books and the book publishing industry that produces them, I don't think I have ever before applied the word "sturdy" to a book. In fact, truth told, I am a little amazed to be doing so now; but amazed or not, I am also reassured by how appropriate and even inevitable "sturdy" feels in its present juxtaposing. But lest there be any confusion, let me define my terms. By using "sturdy" here, I mean to say: this book will wear well because it has a strange kind of candor that seamlessly combines soft intimacy with ecclesial history; this book will walk, quiet and unassuming, through your head and among your activities tomorrow just as profoundly as it does today; this book will sit easy on your heart, although it may at times disturb the rhythms of your day (such, after all, is its stated intention); that this book is sturdy because it is made of sterner stuff than are most books, especially most religion books; this book is about discipline; and this book is a map back to the ancient-future.

Phyllis Tickle
The Farm In Lucy
The Feast of St. Michael and All Angels, 2004

acknowledgements

It seems to me that most authors wait until the end of their preface to say, "Without my spouse this book wouldn't have been possible." On the off chance that you give up on this book before you get there, I'll say it right now: My wife, Julie, is my biggest fan, and if this were a just world, she would have coauthor credits on this book. When I write, it doubles her workload, and yet she steadfastly encourages me and exhorts me onward; and the fact that the due date of our son Aidan coincided almost to the day with the due date of this manuscript only upped the ante. Our children, Tanner, Lily, and days-old Aidan, have also been a blessing. I can't thank the four of them enough.

The majority of the research and writing for the book you're about to read took place while I was on a three-month sabbatical from my pastoral duties at Colonial Church. Having reached my five-year anniversary on staff, the congregation and my coworkers were gracious enough to grant me that time for rest and writing. Further, I was given a generous grant by the Louisville Institute, and I thank them and the Lilly Endowment which funds them. The Louisville grant allowed me to travel to Europe, take Julie on a five-year wedding anniversary trip, visit Fuller and Princeton Seminaries, go on a Sabbath Retreat, and buy dozens and dozens of books. Since that time, I've left the employ of Colonial and have been furthering my theological studies at Princeton Theological Seminary. I've also had the opportunity to speak about and reflect upon many of the practices herein, and I hope those experiences enrich this book.

Numerous individuals were both hospitable and helpful to me on my travels. In England I was taken in by good souls like Jonny Baker, Pete Ward, Andy Freeman, and Dave Tomlinson; and in Dublin I was overwhelmed by the gracious reception I received from Fr. Alan McGuckian and the rest of the staff at the Jesuit Communication Centre. Shane and Andrea Hipps and Jen and Jess Elmquist gave me places to sleep in California, and Kenda Dean warmly welcomed me at Princeton. My co-pilgrims on the Sabbath Retreat at the Villa Maria Center in Frontenac, Minnesota, deeply influenced me. During the writing and rewriting process, I thank Mark Oestreicher, Jay Howver, John Raymond, Lois Swagerty, and Carla Barnhill.

Many thanks also to my good friends on the journey, Brian McLaren, Doug Pagitt, Chris Seay, Tim Keel, Tim Conder, Ivy Beckwith, Rudy Carrasco, Laci Scott, Holly Rankin-Zaher, Mark Scandrette, and Jason Clark. My thanks to individuals who lent their expertise and proofread chapters: Phyllis Tickle, Frederica Matthewes-Green, Fr. Alan McGuckian, Jill Hartwell Geffrion, Fr. Nicholas Speier, Jay Folley, and Pat McKee.

I've been blessed to correspond and speak with dozens of persons who graciously and without expecting any reward offered me ideas, wisdom, and cautions. Although most of you go unnamed here, God knows of your selfless devotion and will use your ideas in unexpectedly beautiful ways.

I humbly offer what follows. I'm sure it contains mistakes and misstatements, foibles and misrepresentations. In those cases, please forgive me. In places where it may seem to you inspired or impressively insightful, I give credit to God's guiding Spirit. These past years have been a tremendous journey in my life, and I know that I'll never be the same. I pray that this little book will be received as a small contribution to the ever-expanding Kingdom of God.

Pax et Bonum,
Tony Jones
Feast of St. Aidan of Lindisfarne
31 August, 2004

PART I:
INTRODUCTION

Orthodox Worship and Icons

Sunday, 2:00 p.m.

This morning the Hippses and I went to St. Anthony's Greek Orthodox Church in Pasadena. Having used the Divine Liturgy of St. Chrysostom, I was quite familiar with the order of the service. Also, my knowledge of Greek was indispensable, for about half of the service was in Greek.

I think that the Divine Liturgy is one of the most beautiful things ever written—it seems that every word is carefully chosen, no throw-away lines. It was sung, except where the congregation joined in for the Lord's Prayer and the Nicene Creed. Both the priest and the choir delivered the liturgy wonderfully.

...So, it was a wonder to me that at 10 a.m., when the liturgy began, there were only five people in the sanctuary, including us. By 11 a.m., when the "preliminaries" were over and the procession to the communion began, the place was nearly full.

What was best of all, I think, was the sun coming through the windows and illuminating the dozens of icons on the iconostasis. There really is something mesmerizing and otherworldly about them.

CHAPTER ONE
The Quest for God

Old habits are hard to break, and no one is easily weaned from his own opinions; but if you rely on your own reasoning and ability rather than on the virtue of submission to Jesus Christ, you will but seldom and slowly attain wisdom. For God wills that we become perfectly obedient to himself, and that we transcend mere reason on the wings of burning love for him.

Thomas à Kempis

I wrote a lot of this book in coffee shops. I was working at one in May when a spring thunderstorm came roiling across the plains of western Minnesota. The table at which I was sitting faced the large parking lot of an adjacent mall. As the wind picked up, the trees started to bend, and then the rain came in almost horizontal sheets.

It being a weekday afternoon, the mall's parking lot was only half full. Way out on the edge was parked a brand new BMW 525i—it didn't even have license plates yet. Someone had parked it far away from all other cars, hoping to avoid the dings and dents of carelessly opened doors.

As the wind gusted, I saw a shopping cart begin to roll, pushed by the storm. Free from the constraints of the Cart Corral, the unmanned missile gained speed, unhindered by obstacles as it wheeled across the slick asphalt.

I saw it coming: The cart seemed to be caught in the tractor beam of the new car—250 yards and closing fast! 200 yards! 150! 100 yards! 50...25...10...5...Impact! That cart smashed right into the side of the as-yet unblemished BMW. I kid you not: there wasn't another car within 100 yards, but that cart was honed right in on its target. Mission accomplished.

It seems to me that God is a lot like that shopping cart—not that God has four wheels and a child safety strap, but that God always seeks us out. No matter how far away we park, and no matter how much we try to avoid bumping into the Divine Creator of the Universe, God finds us and leaves a mark. It's not a search-and-destroy mission; it's a search-and-give life mission. I've found that it's pretty common for God to hunt me down and smack me in the right front quarter panel. I know others share this feeling, hence the continued popularity of Francis Thompson's nineteenth century poem, "The Hound of Heaven," in which the protagonist proclaims,

> *I fled Him, down the nights and down the days;*
> *I fled Him, down the arches of the years;*
> *I fled Him, down the labyrinthine ways*
> *Of my own mind; and in the mist of tears*
> *I hid from Him, and under running laughter.*

And yet, Love pursues, with an "unhurrying chase" at an "unperturbèd pace," and a Voice proclaims, "Naught shelters thee, who wilt not shelter Me." Love wins; God wins, hounding the poem's protagonist toward the gates of heaven, never giving up, in spite of attempts to outrun him.

Now, this is a poem not a theological statement. It would be fairly silly to assert that one can't ignore God. In fact, it hardly needs to be stated that, of the six billion people on this planet, a pretty hefty number disregard God completely. But for a lot of us, Frances Thompson's poem articulates something significant. We have this nagging feeling that God is following us around, nudging us to live justly, and expecting us to talk to him every once in a while.[1]

I guess I'm one of those people; one of those whom God is constantly nagging. Every time I leave God's side, as it were, it's not too long until I feel God tagging right along beside *me*. I can't seem to shake him. Yet having this sense of God's company doesn't necessarily translate to a meaningful spiritual life. I know this because despite my awareness of God's presence, I have spent most of my life trying to figure out what to do about it.

why go ancient?

I was raised in a nice, Midwestern, church-going family. I went away to college and got involved in a conservative evangelical college group then went straight to seminary after graduation. In other words, by the time I was 25, my views of God, prayer, the Bible, etc. were pretty screwed up. I had more head-knowledge about faith, religion, whatever you want to call it, than a person should, but I really didn't seem to be able to put it into practice. I'd say there was one word that summed up my religious life: *obligation*.

I had been taught that the way to connect with God on a daily basis is to have a 30-minute "quiet time." That is, you should sit down with your Bible open, read it a little, and then lay a bunch of stuff on God, making sure to mention how excellent he[1] is before running through the list of all the things you need.

I found this style of personal devotion to be a pretty shallow well, and it wasn't long before I was doing it only every other day, then once a week, and then, well, never. Taking the place of my 30-minute quiet time, however, were hours and hours of that great religious tradition: guilt. Here was the equation: God is out there + God wants to hear from me + I'm not talking = failure by me.

After about 10 years of this, and hearing this same pattern corroborated by many people who were also trying to listen for God in their lives, something occurred to me: people have been trying to follow God for thousands of years, Christians for the last two thousand. Maybe somewhere along the line some of them had come up with ways of connecting with God that could help people like me.

---

[1] I feel very uncomfortable referring to God as "he." On the one hand, I strongly believe that God is a personal being, but on the other hand, I believe that God is so much more than our words "he," "she," "him," and "her" can capture. Recently, I've been trying to explain this to my 3- and 4-year-olds. When they look around at other people, dogs, birds, and hamsters, they only know "he" and "she," so trying to convince them that God is neither and both and more than the two combined has been a challenge. So in this book, I'll try to avoid references to God as "he" or "she," but sometimes I'll have to break my own rule in order to avoid literary awkwardness.

About that same time, I happened to be due for a three-month sabbatical from my job, and I could think of no better way to spend it than to travel and read about different ancient ways of prayer and devotion. So that's exactly what I did.

My travels took me to England, where I stayed at the now defunct Boiler Room in Reading, a prayer center for young people. Some churches there got together and leased out an abandoned pub, which happened to sit on the site of a medieval abbey destroyed during the Protestant-Catholic tensions of the sixteenth century. The churches wanted to develop a place where the young people of Reading could come and hang out, but instead of filling the old pub with pinball games and loud music, those in charge constructed prayer chapels and piped in ethereal chants. While it was open (2000-2003), the Reading Boiler Room boasted a 24-hours-a-day, 7-days-a-week prayer vigil, and people from around the world posted prayer requests on the "Wailing Wall" on their website. A new Boiler Room has since been opened in West London, and other branches of the British 24-7 prayer movement are being launched as well.

I also flew to Dublin, Ireland, where I met with Fr. Alan Mc-Guckian and the staff at the Jesuit Communication Centre, the keepers of the most popular prayer website in the world (you can read more about it in chapter 8). And I went to Communaute Taizé, an amazing community of peace, brotherhood, and prayer in southern France (see more in chapter 11).

I voraciously read authors and books they didn't assign in seminary: St. John of the Cross, St. Theresa of Avila, and *The Pilgrim's Way*. I met with other Protestants, with Roman Catholics, and with Eastern Orthodox Christians. I took a long hike in the Red Mountains of Utah with a shaman. I corresponded by e-mail with people around the world, and I talked with others about prayer over the phone.

All this I did in an effort to solve my dilemma. For years I'd been told that to be a Christian meant I had to do three things: (1) read the Bible, (2) pray, and (3) go to church. But I had come to the realization that there must be something *more*. And indeed there is. There is a long tradition of searching among the followers of Jesus—it's a quest, really, for ways to connect with God— and it has been undertaken by some of the most intelligent and deeply spiritual persons ever to walk this planet. The quest is to know Jesus better, to follow him more closely, to become—in some mysterious way—wrapped into his presence. And I thank

God that some of these brilliant and spiritual persons wrote down what they learned.

For me, there is incredible richness in the spiritual practices of ancient and modern Christian communities from around the world. Incorporating new ways of praying, meditating, reading the Bible, etc. have fueled my faith and my passion for spirituality in ways I never thought possible, and have, without question, brought me into a closer relationship with God. And beyond those rather self-centered outcomes, they've also helped me to become a better father, husband, and friend. And that's why I'm interested in writing about them as an offering to you.

why christian?

You've probably noticed that for me, the point of these practices is to draw me into a deeper relationship with the Christian God. You may or may not agree that spirituality necessarily involves God. Obviously, I feel strongly that the road to inner peace and connection with our Creator is through Jesus. If you are one of the more than two billion Christians in the world, you may feel the same way. But in case you don't, I think you'll still find a great deal of worthy information here. I'm not going to try to convince you that you can only do these things if you believe in Jesus — I've seen lots of people try to convince other people about Jesus, and it's rarely successful.

Instead, I suggest you try some of these spiritual practices with an open mind. Honestly, what have you got to lose? Even if you already count yourself among those convinced of the whole Christian thing, you may remain skeptical about the part where Jesus talks to you. (If you're like me, you get more than a little uneasy when your coworker says that when she was late for her son's soccer game, the Lord helped her find a great parking spot; or when your brother says the Lord told him to do this or that. The Lord just doesn't speak to me like that.)

So if you're unconvinced, or convinced but still skeptical, or even if you're a stalwart Christian who has a stale prayer life, the exercises in this book may prove helpful.

The funny thing is, I can't really tell you *why* they're helpful. I know they work because they have for me, but I'm still confounded by their effectiveness. Maybe it's because the ancient spiritual disciplines cause us to slow down and shut up, something at which most of us are not very good. Maybe it's that there's something mystical and mysterious about these ancient rites, like we're tapping into some pretechnological, preindustrial treasury of the Spirit.

But I think they work because of Jesus. I'm afraid you're not going to get much more explanation from me than that. Still, I think that something about Jesus—who he was (Jesus of Nazareth) and who he is (Jesus the Christ)—inspired the people who developed these disciplines centuries ago. He led them on this quest, which really is unique to Christianity. For only in Christianity is there the belief that the one, true God came to earth as a human being, and that, to this day, we can know him in as personal a way as the disciples who shared lunch with him 2,000 years ago. That is, Christians engage in these spiritual practices not out of duty or obligation but because there is a promise attached: God will personally meet us in the midst of these disciplines.

It's really pretty crazy when you think about it—which is probably why some of the saints who favored these disciplines were driven to extremes that their contemporaries considered mad. (St. Francis preached to the birds in the forest—in the nude; Benedict's disciples tried to poison him because he was too strict about prayer; Julian of Norwich had herself walled into a little apartment for years with food thrown in to her once a day through a hole in the roof; the Stylites sat on tall poles for years at a time.) Despite their sometimes-odd methods, the passion with which these saints followed Jesus might be envied by us today. In our age of cynicism in which everything falls prey to deconstruction, it's inspiring to look back to an age before Newton explained how the world works and Freud explained how the psyche works. Following these saints' lead, of pouring oneself into something without really understanding it, can be an incredibly liberating experience. It has been for me.

Imagine thinking about spirituality in a time when the words of Jesus had not been picked apart and voted on by the Jesus Seminar; the veracity of Jesus' miracles had not been analyzed by *Time* Magazine; his sexuality had not been the subject of movies and plays. Having not experienced the cynicism of our postmodern age, the ancient saints pursued Jesus with a relentlessness we can hardly imagine—not all of them, to be sure, but enough of them to make the history of Christian spirituality one of the most fascinating fields in historical study.

And again, I submit that all this took place *because of Jesus*. In the end, there is something so compelling about the person of Jesus and the way of life he offers that it causes people to commit everything to the pursuit of him and his way. Many are saying that right now is a time where the spiritual quest for Jesus is again on the rise—that people are tired of Jesus being hoarded by the academicians, that we want him back as Lord and Friend.

But is it cheating for us to jump backwards, to look for spiritual guidance to the era before the Enlightenment? Only if we look back with nostalgia, like the people who say, "I would have fit much better during the Renaissance than now," or the people who spend all their time and money on Civil War reenactments. On the contrary, traditional Christian practice is not about nostalgia, but about a way of life and faith that has been honed by the centuries. It is a way—*the* way—to live in the sacredness of God.

why me?

Because so many of the spiritual disciplines in this book were developed and practiced by those we now consider saints, there can be a sense of exclusivity, a belief that these are only for the deeply devout or those who are prepared to drastically alter their lives—to live in solitude, fast for months at a time, or give up all worldly possessions. But my hope is that you see them as truly practical ways of awakening your spiritual life. It may be a cliché, but if I can do it, you can too.

You'll be either disillusioned or relieved to discover that I am not a spiritual guru (whatever that means). I'm not a monk, I don't live on a mountain, and I rarely wear robes. Instead, I'm a husband, father, brother, son, and friend. I'm trying to make a living, stay in shape, and finish reading the novel I started two months ago.

This book wasn't written high in the Himalayas while I lived on crusts of bread and honey. I wrote some of it in coffee shops and much of it on a folding table in the middle of the half-painted nursery for our new baby.

I say this not out of some false sense of humility, but to make the point that you and I are probably very much alike in our quest for God. I truly struggle to make time for God every day, and I struggle to set an example for my children. I can imagine them someday saying, "My dad writes books on spirituality, but let me tell you what he's *really* like at home!"

In the end, following Jesus is not easy, and those who portray it as easy are doing all of us a disservice. It's in fact a very difficult journey, and it's quite easy to give it up, even on the most mundane days. So I would hope this confession gives you hope, and that you see that the writings in this book are simply the scrawls of one journeyer to another.

about this book

For that reason, the following chapters are pretty thin when it comes to how-to. To be honest, I don't really know how you're best going to achieve intimacy with God. I know what's worked for me, and I'll try to indicate that along the way. But please don't take my experimentation with these practices as prescriptive; they are merely descriptive of my wanderings. Yours will be yours.

That said, one of the things you may have to leave at the front cover is any denominational bigotry you have. A lot of the practices herein will seem very "Catholic" or very "Eastern Ortho-dox." If you aren't from one of those traditions and feel wary about adopting practices associated with them, remember this: Before 1054, all Christians were Catholic/Orthodox! That's right, for the first half of Christian history, there was one church and most of the practices in this book are from that time.

The next chapter is further introduction, including thoughts on spirituality and the practice thereof. Then comes the meat of the book: 16 ancient practices. The practices are divided into two sections. Those in *Via Contemplativa* are practices that rely on bodily quiet and stillness. For most of them you sit, and for all of them you primarily engage the Spirit of God via your own spirit. The following section, *Via Activa*, describes practices in which you engage your body, whether it be by depriving it of food (e.g., fasting) or walking (e.g., Stations of the Cross).

While this division of body and spirit, and the corresponding disciplines, is ancient, it's also a false dichotomy. To practice the stillness required for Centering Prayer, for example, takes an enormous amount of physical discipline—one must use the mind/brain (a physical organ) to bring the body to rest and to tune out all possible distractions. And to walk a labyrinth, though it is physical, is also deeply spiritual. However artificial, the division stands for it may be somewhat helpful.

Each chapter begins with a quote from Thomas à Kempis's *The Imitation of Christ*, quite possibly the greatest, and surely the most widely read Christian spiritual classic after the Bible. It is a truly astounding book of spiritual insight, as I think you will see from the quotes I've chosen. I hope they pique your curiosity enough to get a copy and devour it yourself.

Each chapter also has several sections. The first is an opening anecdote, either from my own life or, more often, from someone else's. Hopefully, these stories will bring the practice to life and pull you into its snare.

Next is a section on the history of the practice, not only because I love history, but also because we do a great disservice to a discipline and to the faithful Christians who have practiced it when we do not consider from whence it came. Indeed, I find that many people are far more interested in trying a practice when they know the story behind it.

Theology is the next part of each chapter. In order for us to practice these spiritual disciplines with integrity, we must decide for ourselves if they are theologically defensible within our own traditions. The use of icons for prayer, for instance, has a long and contentious theological history. And the labyrinth, because of its pre-Christian origins and its use by the New Age movement, is avoided by some Christians. Obviously, I have included no practices with which I am theologically uncomfortable, but you will have to make those determinations for yourself.

Next is a section on practice, giving some general guidelines for the application of the discipline. These have been honed over the centuries by thousands of Christians, but I have found that all are adaptable to our present-day lives where we have jobs and family responsibilities.

Finally, since I don't deserve to have the last word on any of these disciplines, there is a word from someone much wiser than I to conclude each chapter. Then it's your turn: try them, experiment, dive in, and see where God takes you.

A final word

Here's our first "Final Word;" consider it a blessing and exhortation as you finish the chapter.

In 1373, when she was 30 years old, Benedictine nun Julian of Norwich (1342–ca.1416) received 16 "showings," or revelations from God. She spent the rest of her life in seclusion, reflecting on her visions. Years later she dictated her visions and her interpretations to a scribe who wrote them down. They are now considered the height of late medieval Christian mysticism. She's notable for her optimism, for her emphasis on the motherly qualities of Christ, and for her supreme confidence in God's love. Here's a word of encouragement from Julian:

*Therefore we can with his grace and his help persevere in spiritual
contemplation, with endless wonder at this high, surpassing, immeasurable love
which our Lord in his goodness has for us; and therefore we may with reverence
ask from our lover all that we will, for our natural will is to have God, and
God's good will is to have us, and we can never stop willing or loving
until we possess him in the fullness of joy.*

Journaling

I've taken about a week off from writing in my journal. There are a couple reasons: 1) last week was spent at a spa with Julie celebrating our anniversary, and I really wanted to show her in my actions that she's the most important thing to me—more important than a book and more important than my journal. Not that the two are mutually exclusive (they're not) or that she would have resented me writing (she wouldn't have)—it's just a statement I wanted to make.

And 2) I realize that I tend toward obsessiveness, in thought and deed. Once I decide to do something, almost nothing can convince me to do otherwise. I also have a tendency to quit something if I don't do it perfectly. I once read that major league managers routinely have players sit out a game (early on in their careers) so they won't be tempted to try breaking Cal Ripkin Jr.'s consecutive game record. That kind of record can become a prison.

In the same way, a spiritual discipline can be a prison. The first time I missed the Daily Office after having "religiously" fulfilled it for a couple weeks, I felt like a failure. Part of my journey is going to have to be learning grace for myself. The disciplines should be freedom, not bondage.

I'm on a plane to L.A. This is the trip I'm least looking forward to—I miss my kids horribly, and I have a seven-day trip right on the heels of this one—but I pray that God will cause some incredible things to happen in my time here.

CHAPTER TWO
what is spirituality and HOW DO YOU practice it?

If you wish to live in peace and harmony with others, you must learn to discipline yourself in many ways.

Thomas à Kempis

The term *spirituality* has gotten a bad reputation among some people. Maybe it's the fact that since the Enlightenment, intellectual knowledge, theology, and doctrine have been the primary means by which people come to enter the religious life. Maybe it's because the term was co-opted by the New Age movement in the late twentieth century. Whatever the reason, some Christians, evangelicals foremost among them, have shied away from this word.

Yet others love the word. To them it connotes the best of the relationship between humanity and the Divine without all the negative aspects of organized religion. Ask any random group of people, and inevitably you'll find that nearly a third of them will say, "I'm not religious, but I'm a very spiritual person." This, of course, is a somewhat misleading statement, for religion is simply human beings' attempts to sort out the ways in which we seek after God. Sometimes we've done that well, other times poorly.

It's no wonder, then, that there is some risk in writing about spirituality; it's hard to know what kind of baggage readers bring with them when they come to a book intended to deepen their spiritual lives. So I'd like to offer a sense of what I mean by spirituality. Naturally, there are any number of definitions, but since all of the practices outlined in this book grow out of the Christian tradition, I will focus on a few of the most common definitions of Christian spirituality.

- A fairly academic definition comes from Alister McGrath: "Christian spirituality concerns the quest for a fulfilled and authentic Christian existence, involving the bringing together of the fundamental ideas of Christianity and the whole experience of living on the basis of and within the scope of the Christian faith."
- Presbyterian pastor Marjorie Thompson prefers the more biblical phrase, "the spiritual life," which she describes as "simply the increasing vitality and sway of God's Spirit in us."
- Seventeenth-century mystic Brother Lawrence had a definition that's simpler yet: "the practice of the presence of God."

Spirituality is derived from the word "spirit" (*ruach* in the Hebrew Old Testament, *pneuma* in the Greek New Testament, and *spiritus* in Latin — all of these primarily mean "breath"), so it clearly has connections with God's Holy Spirit, the third person of the Christian Trinity. The Spirit hovered over the face of the waters at the genesis of the world, gave Jesus his power to heal, gave birth to the church at Pentecost, and dwells with believers as the "Advocate" that Jesus promised.

So here's my own attempt at a definition: *The goal of Christian spirituality is to be enlivened by God's Spirit.*

No matter one's theological disposition, it's clear the protagonist in this relationship is God. In the gospel of John, Jesus tells a Pharisee named Nicodemus that God's Spirit is like the wind — we know it's there, but we don't know where it came from or where it's going. The Spirit moves at God's whim, and, as the Lord reminded the Old Testament figure, Job, God's ways are often incomprehensible to mortals. The history of revivals (in all Christian traditions) points to one fact: when and where the Holy Spirit moves is neither predictable nor controllable. That's why I've written my one-sentence definition of Christian spirituality in the passive voice: "*To be* enlivened by God's Spirit." That is, it is God's Spirit who gives us spiritual life; it is not ours to attain, achieve, or earn. God is the giver, and we are the recipients.

A Relationship

However, we human beings do have a role. For a unique aspect of Christianity is that because of Jesus Christ and the Holy Spirit, we have a relationship with the Creator of the cosmos. Marjorie Thompson's definition of the spiritual life goes on: "It is a magnificent choreography of the Holy Spirit in the human spirit, moving us toward communion with both Creator and creation. The spiritual life is thus grounded in relationship. It has to do with God's way of relating to us and our way of responding to God."

Human beings play an active role in spirituality, for we seek to come inside or under God's Spirit—or to have God's Spirit come inside us to dwell. All of the interest in spirituality and religion (organized or unorganized) is a result of what Blaise Pascal called the "infinite abyss" within each of us, which "can only be filled by an infinite and immutable object, that is to say, only by God himself." While some of us may scoff at today's upstart religions, cults, sects, and gurus, they are popular and successful because people are *seeking*. People want, as Thompson writes, communion with the Creator and the creation.

In this way, Christians are no different than any other group or individual—we're on a quest, we're seekers. Those Christians who walk around smug in their certainty that they've got it all figured out, that the quest is over, might well hear Jesus' words to Peter ringing in their ears: "Get behind me, Satan!" It is a dangerous conceit to believe that we can ever be one with the Spirit of God, that the quest for God has an end point, that you can have "success." Actually, it should come as no surprise that the Christian faith is more of a quest than a destination, for Jesus himself was a wanderer, the most famous peripatetic pilgrim ever to strap on a pair of sandals. And since the time of Jesus, the quest for God has only intensified as human beings have discovered more about our minds and bodies, our planet, and our universe.

This search has driven countless men and women into the desert—we know them as the Desert Fathers and Mothers. It has driven others into monasteries and convents. Others have gone to the mission field or into a cave or into a commune or climbed a pole to pursue a deeper communion with God. Some have sought it in a community, others in seclusion.

Our age is no different. We are, if you believe the newsmagazines, a nation of seekers. Many churches have capitalized on this sensibility, as have several different strains of Buddhism. The media—and the church to some degree—tend to treat this surge in spiritual seeking as a new trend. But at the risk of repeating myself: people have been seeking after God for as long as there've been people.

A Rich Diversity

It is in the process of this age-old journey that individuals and communities developed the spiritual practices of the Christian tradition in order to seek greater communion with God. As a result, Christian spiritual practices vary widely, heavily influenced by the people and times in which they were forged. They also reflect the often-tumultuous history of the Christian church. While the divisions within the Christian church are mainly tragic, the splits between East and West in 1054 and between Protestant and Roman Catholic in 1517 also led to a rich diversity in the field of spirituality. Each tradition has developed its own practices, and every practice carries the fingerprint of the milieu in which it was conceived. While some of these disciplines were virtually unknown across denominational lines for centuries, we now live in a time of unprecedented cross-pollination.

The Roman Catholic Church, for example, places much emphasis on liturgy and the sacraments. For this reason, practices like the Stations of the Cross developed as a part of the sacrament of confession, and the Daily Office is, at its heart, a way to order the day liturgically. Even the labyrinth, as it was originally conceived, was to be walked as preparation for receiving the Eucharist. The Catholic Church also boasts those most responsible for the worldwide development of monasteries and, consequently, the disciplines that began therein.

The Orthodox Church is known to us most specifically in its Greek, Russian, and Antiochian forms. These all share a spiritual tradition of *hesychasm* (from the Greek word for 'quietness'). The hesychasts, dating back to the fourth century, are monks who

have taught that the way to enter God's Divine Light is prayer
of absolute quiet, in which the heart and the mind become one.
Centering Prayer and the Jesus Prayer are two examples of this
type of prayer. Orthodox spirituality also relies heavily upon
praying with icons, an adjunct of their theological emphasis on
Jesus' incarnation, and a tradition that is quite unfamiliar to most
Western Christians.

Protestantism, the latest movement on the scene, currently has
two distinct streams within it. Mainline Protestant spirituality is
a roll-up-your-sleeves spirituality, with much emphasis on action,
social justice, and bringing about the Kingdom of God on earth.
Evangelical spirituality is guided more by personal Bible study
and devotion, free-form prayer, and personal conversion to a relationship with Jesus Christ.

All three of these traditions have added significantly to the
depth and breadth of spiritual practices available to Christians. Indeed, a well-rounded believer of any denomination could do worse
than committing to practice one discipline from each tradition.

The practice

You've already noticed that I'm using terms such as "practice"
and "discipline" when it comes to Christian spirituality, terms
more often connected to the cello or sitting in the principal's
office. But in fact, these are key concepts in the two-millennia
trajectory of the Christian tradition. For instance, in a letter to the
church in Corinth, the Apostle Paul used a metaphor to describe
the Christian life:

> Do you not know that in a race the runners all compete, but only one receives the
> prize? Run in such a way that you may win it. Athletes exercise self-control in
> all things; they do it to receive a perishable wreath, but we an imperishable one.
> So I do not run aimlessly, nor do I box as though beating the air; but I punish
> my body and enslave it, so that after proclaiming to others I myself should not
> be disqualified.

Ever since, athletic imagery has been common in describing the
pursuit of a life with God. In English, words like *discipline*, *practice*,
and *exercise* are common metaphors for faith-related activities.
In Greek, the word is *askesis* (as-kée-sis), translated "exercise,"
or "training." Asceticism was common among the ancient Greek
moral philosophers who encouraged moral training through
avoidance of fleshly pleasures; a similar concept is a guiding force

in the wisdom literature of the Old Testament. When comparing the daily life of a Christian to carrying a cross, Jesus launched ascetical theology, and Paul wrote often about the need to be disciplined in the Christian life.

There are two sides to the coin of asceticism. On the negative side is self-abnegation—the discipline to practice restraint, moderation, and self-denial. Gregory of Sinai (d. 1360), a Desert Father, gives voice to this emphasis:

> *One thing more I have to add from my own experience: a monk can in no way succeed without the following virtues: fasting, abstinence, vigil, patience, courage, silence, prayer, not talking, tears, humility, which generate and preserve one another. Constant fasting withers lust, and gives birth to abstinence; abstinence to vigil; vigil to patience; patience to courage; courage to silence; silence to prayer; prayer to abstinence from talk; abstinence from talk to weeping; weeping to humility; humility again to weeping, and so on.*

Ascetic disciplines have been commonly practiced in the church since the early centuries. Orders of monks were gathered around vows of celibacy and poverty, and the Desert Fathers and Mothers often practiced silence and fasting. Particularly in the Eastern Church, this is related to *apophatic* theology (also known as *negative theology*), the idea that any human conceptions of God (including language) are inadequate. Thus, the only way we can really achieve union with God is by ceasing all ideas and all language, and only then approaching God in emptiness (i.e., silence and fasting).

The positive side of asceticism is following Christ—striving after him. It's this movement that Paul invokes when he uses athletic imagery. While an athlete may prepare for a race by refraining from fatty foods and alcohol and getting plenty of sleep, eventually the race comes and the athlete must take the initiative to leave the starting blocks and run the course.

Christian writer Kathleen Norris writes, "Asceticism reminds us that our time, and our bodies, are not truly our own….The command comes out loud and clear: *be here, now*. And the demands of the body, the whining of the self, recede into the background." In other words, disciplining the body and the mind by way of spiritual practices aids us in focusing on *what really matters* in life: being loved by God, serving God, and serving others.

practice, practice, practice

If there's a common theme among the great Christian spiritual writers, it's this: *Seeking God will not be easy.* The history of the church is the story of many faithful Christians admirably fighting back their own sins by these disciplines, only to be thwarted again and again. But, as with a sport, the more you practice, the better you get. You'll get in better "spiritual shape" as you practice, and you'll be able to run the race to completion…even "in such a way that you may win it!"

In fact, the athletic metaphor can be pushed even further. A common theme in modern Christianity has been that head knowledge is how one becomes more adept at following Christ: the more you know, the better you'll do. But in fact, that hasn't proven to be true.

Instead, it seems that the Christian life is more like being a baseball shortstop: A young player can watch videos, read books by the greatest shortstops of all time, and listen to coaches lecture on what makes a good shortstop; but what will make him a truly good shortstop is getting out on the field and practicing. The only way he'll really get a feel for the game is to field ground ball after ground ball, to figure out when to play the ball on a short hop, how to get his whole body in front of it, why he needs to cheat over when a pull-hitter is at bat, and how far to cheat toward second base when the double play is on. The more practice he has, the better he'll be.

Getting a "feel for the game" in following Jesus is much the same. You can listen to innumerable sermons and read countless books, but the true transformation happens only when you practice the disciplines that lie at the heart of faith. As the disciplines are practiced, your life becomes more attuned to God's life, and you become more "at one" with the rhythms of creation. Like a finely trained athlete, you can anticipate the movement on the field; like a world-class pianist, you actually inhabit the music as you take notes on the page and give them life; like an expert carpenter, you run your hands over the grain of the wood and see what this rough cut can become.

All of these examples demand practice, and I propose you begin to imagine the Christian life in much the same way. You've probably had some experience practicing an instrument, or working out in a committed way, or becoming better and better at chess. Take the same commitment to practice you used in that endeavor and apply it to one or two of the spiritual disciplines in this book. In the words of the trainer at your health club, I guarantee results! And these results are far more significant than bigger biceps or a flatter stomach.

There is a noteworthy difference, however, between athletic discipline and the Christian spiritual life. While athletic practice makes us stronger, physically and mentally so we're more present during a competition, spiritual discipline means making less of ourselves so we can be more aware of what God is up to. Henri Nouwen said,

> *In the spiritual life, the word "discipline" means "the effort to create some space in which God can act." Discipline means to prevent everything in your life from being filled up. Discipline means that somewhere you're not occupied, and certainly not preoccupied. In the spiritual life, discipline means to create that space in which something can happen that you hadn't planned or counted on.*

The promise

So there's the payoff: "something you hadn't planned or counted on." Unlike a lot of the self-help style Christian books available today, I don't promise you any tangible earthly rewards. I can't tell you your territory will increase or that your purpose in life will become crystal clear.

I'm actually after something else — something far more valuable: *fire*. That's the image used again and again by the Christian mystics. That is, while the spiritual disciplines are often mundane chores, once in a while God's Spirit engulfs us with a holy passion. When it happens, it's pure gift. It is not to be expected or invoked. It is in these moments of mystical union with Christ that our true purpose in life is revealed.

A final word

Abba Joseph of Panephysis lived in the desert in the fifth century. He recorded this conversation between two of his fellow Desert Fathers:

> *Abba Lot went to see Abba Joseph and said to him, "Abba, as far as I can, I say my little office, I fast a little, I pray and meditate, I live in peace and as far as I can, I purify my thoughts. What else can I do?" Then the old man stood up and stretched his hands toward heaven. His fingers became like ten lamps of fire and he said to him, "If you will, you can become all flame."*

PART II:
VIA CONTEMPLATIVA:
contemplative
APPROACHES TO
SPIRITUALITY

Pilgrimage

I'm making my way to Taizé on the TGV. Last night was one of those dinners that epitomizes Paris. I checked into a fairly seedy hotel around 8:30 p.m. and made my way to a guidebook-recommended restaurant. It was, of course, still half-empty at 9 p.m. It took about 20 minutes to even get a menu, and then the meal itself took about two and a half hours. Fortunately I had brought the Herald Tribune, and it took me about that long to get all the way through it.

I tried to get up early enough to run along the Seine, but I just couldn't do it. I'm still feeling worn down, and I look forward to getting home in three days.

I imagine two things about ancient and medieval Christian pilgrims as compared to my pilgrimage to Taizé: I'll bet they were both more and less lonely than I am. Having now passed the week point of being gone from home, compounded by a country where few speak my language, a rainy and cold day, and no one here being all that welcoming, I've hit the wall. It's nowhere near the loneliness I have felt while traveling in Europe in the past, but it's still not a good feeling.

3 p.m.: I got put in a room with a bunch of Germans who, even after hearing that I only know English, continued to speak German. And the food sucks. No, seriously, it's slop on a plastic tray.

Which leads me back to the difference between me and the medievals. When a person in the Middle Ages set off on a pilgrimage, it took months or even years. For me it took hours/days. For them it was on foot—some, like St. Ignatius, walked barefoot to Jerusalem. For me, today was a combination of planes, trains, and buses. I did face some hardship, though, when my bag flew out of the bus's luggage bay on a roundabout.

For them, the whole village would have come to see them off, given them money and food for the journey, and prayed for them with constancy. For me, my family drove me to the airport.

But the biggest difference must be that pilgrims in the Middle Ages were conspicuous. They wore a cloak with patches of saints on them and they carried a special staff that denoted their pilgrimage. For those reasons, people took them in and gave them food, shelter, and money. In return, the pilgrim would offer to pray for those who helped him and to offer special prayers on their behalf when he arrived at the holy site.

While the people I have met with know I'm on a pilgrimage, the old lady who owned the seedy hotel where I stayed in Paris didn't. Neither did the nice young man who ran the hotel in London—he told me to be sure and go to the Moulin Rouge while I was in Paris. And the bus driver showed me no special grace when my bag rolled out of the bus.

So I guess it's good and bad. On the one hand, pilgrimages aren't nearly as costly (finances, time, health, death) as they used to be, but with their ease, we've lost something, too.

chapter three
silence and solitude

In silence and quietness the devout soul makes progress and learns the hidden mysteries of the Scriptures.

Thomas à Kempis

Adam Cleavland is a seminary student, an avid blogger (http://cleave.blogs.com/pomomusings), and a friend of mine:

> Over the course of my life, I've been blessed to have met and spent time with scholarly German monks, monks in Idaho who keep watch over chickens, and reclusive monks who love to hike throughout the desert cliffs of northern New Mexico. While their languages, hobbies, and chores may differ, all these monks absolutely intrigue me, for they have the ability, desire, and strength to do what I can rarely do: live and find peace in solitude.
>
> Our technology-driven world seeks to worship the god of multitasking. We bemoan the added nuisances that technology brings, yet we seem-

ingly can't live without its benefits. We have, in fact, become slaves to our computers, PDAs, and all things WiFi. We claim to want to "just get away from it all" for a while. Some choose remote beaches or the wilderness, while others seek out the serenity of the ocean coast; I choose the monastery.

While working in southern Idaho, after spending the afternoon with extremely energetic elementary students, I realized something: "I need solitude. I need time to refocus, to realign myself with what God desires for me. I need silence and stillness." So I made it a habit to get away at least once every few months and spend time at the Monastery of the Ascension in Jerome, Idaho. I went, and it was hard. I was in a small room—my cell phone turned off and placed in a drawer—and left alone with my Bible, a journal, and the silence of the guest quarters. All of a sudden, I became nervous. *What now? What am I supposed to do...?* Finally, I had what I wanted: a temporary escape from my never-ending to-do list, from my cell phone, from e-mail, from noisy kids running around in the church—just me and God. And I suddenly became scared: I didn't know what to do.

I began to read from the Psalms, a bit from Ezekiel, some gospel words of Jesus. I sat down and tried to journal for a bit. I found it difficult to be focused, to align myself with the things of God that I was supposed to find so clearly here in the monastery. Immediately, I had a profound respect and admiration for those monks who have committed their lives to at least some form of solitude and journey toward the face of God. Their lives intrigue me, for they can do what I long for, what I struggle with, and what I so often cannot do: focus and find peace in solitude.

There is something about solitude and silence, something that makes them both desirable and awe-ful. I fear the silence. I fear that God won't speak. I fear what I may hear, or that I may not hear. Trappist monk Thomas Merton wrote in his *Thoughts in Solitude*, "My life is listening, His is speaking. My salvation is to hear and respond. For this, my life must be silent. Hence, my silence is my salvation." That evening I spent at the monastery, I realized I needed silence. I'd been focusing on *doing*, and I needed to redirect my focus and allow myself to abide in Jesus: I needed to allow myself to *be*. It wasn't easy. I glanced at a few verses, put everything away, and got into a comfortable position sitting up on my bed. After a while I was able to quiet myself, my mind, my soul, and simply enter into a time of being in God's presence. What follows is an excerpt from my journal following that experience:

As I lay there, just repeating the phrase, God's abounding love, I simply became peaceful. I became very aware of each breath I took in through my nose. I could feel it going deep inside me. I felt as though I was in a deep state of peace and relaxation. There was nothing wrong with the moment. I felt like I understood, just for a moment, a small fraction of God's abounding love. Maybe it was not even an understanding…but I felt God's love—and that was a beautiful thing.

For those few moments, silence and solitude were not frightening or awkward. They were, instead, my gateway into the peace of the presence of God.

HISTORY

"The tongue has the power of life and death, and those who love it will eat its fruit." So says the wise author of Proverbs, and many places within the Hebrew and Christian Scriptures stand in agreement. Ancient philosophers of all stripes agree—their consensus is that to speak much is a vice and to keep silent is a virtue. Of course, Jesus spent time talking and teaching, but he also valued his times of silence and solitude, seeking space for prayer, reflection, and respite in times of distress. The *Catholic Encyclopedia* emphatically states, "All writers on the spiritual life uniformly recommend, nay, command under penalty of total failure, the practice of silence."

All in all, no spiritual discipline is more universally acclaimed as necessary than the practice of silence. The Desert Fathers retreated to the wild lands of Egypt; Rufinus, who toured the desert to visit as many of the Fathers as he could, wrote to Jerome, "This is the utter desert where each monk remains alone in his cell…There is a huge silence and a great quiet here." In fact, as more and more pilgrims like Rufinus crowded the desert to pester the Fathers, the desert monks withdrew into deeper parts of the wilderness to find the quiet they desired.

Likewise, Benedict fashioned much of his *Rule* around the keeping of silence. When talking is allowed, it's to be done with charity and moderation; useless and idle words are always forbidden. Areas of the monastery exist where talking is necessary and permitted, but in other areas and at certain times of the day, silence is strictly observed. And after Compline—the last prayer service of the day—the Great Silence is kept until prayers the next morning.

Present day spiritual writers commend silence as well. Richard Foster carries on the tradition, linking silence and solitude: "Without silence there is no solitude. Though silence sometimes involves the absence of speech, it always involves the act of listening. Simply to refrain from talking, without a heart listening to God, is not silence."

Ultimately, we keep silence and solitude so we can listen better—so we can hear what God is saying to us and to our world. It's like being on the phone with a friend who has something important to tell me. I will move out of the noisy room where the TV is on and the vacuum is running and shut myself in a closet so I can really hear what my friend is saying. That's the kind of attentive listening silence and solitude engender.

Theology

The tradition that Foster continues, coupling solitude and silence, goes back at least to Jesus. In preparation for his ministry, Jesus spent 40 days in the wilderness outside of Jerusalem, setting the example for the monks who would follow him there three centuries later. Clearly in solitude, Jesus was presumably in silence as well, talking only to his *Abba*, his 'Poppa'—and, finally, rebuffing Satan.

From then on, Jesus made a habit of withdrawing to "the hills" or "a lonely place" or "the wilderness" or "a high mountain" or the Garden of Gethsemene. He went to these places before he chose his disciples, after he heard of his cousin John's beheading, after feeding the 5000, after healing a leper, before the transfiguration, and, of course, to prepare for his passion. Richard Foster says, "The seeking out of solitary places was a regular practice for Jesus. So it should be for us."

But what do silence and solitude actually accomplish in us? When I informally poll my friends, I find that most of them have no silence and little solitude in their lives. They are awakened by a clock radio, eat breakfast to morning television, drive to school or work with music, talk most of the day to friends, schoolmates, and coworkers, listen to music on the way home, have the TV on while they prepare dinner, eat dinner with the TV on, watch a movie or their favorite show, and fall asleep with music playing. Ours is a life filled with noise.

I also talk to many individuals who feel depressed or are even suffering from diagnosed, clinical depression. Many factors contribute to this, but one fact is noticeable: all the noise and all the talking does not quell a major symptom of this depression — loneliness. Although we are surrounded by the stimuli of music, television, and conversation (both personal and virtual), we often feel disconnected from other people, from God, and, ultimately from ourselves.

Spiritual writers, ancient and modern, are unanimous in saying that silence and solitude lead to a love of God, a love of self, and a love of others. In the 430s, Abba Arsenius lived in the desert. Prior to this, while living in a palace, he asked God how he could be led in the way of salvation, and a voice answered him, "Arsenius, flee from men and you will be saved." Once in the desert, he prayed the same prayer and this time he heard, "Arsenius, flee, be silent, pray always, for these are the source of sinlessness."

The reason Christians are to seek silence and solitude above all else is for the same reason Jesus did: to be able to hear from God. John Climacus (ca.570-ca.649), a Desert Father, wrote in his classic *The Ladder of Divine Ascent*, "The lover of silence draws close to God. He talks to him in secret and God enlightens him." Humble silence opens the ears and causes the listener to hear that "sound of sheer silence" in which God so often speaks.

Another reason to practice silence and solitude is to discover what we can learn from ourselves when we turn off the external stimuli that are so much a part of our world. Interestingly, that silence often leads to what one medieval writer, St. John of the Cross (1542-1591), called "the dark night of the soul." It seems one cannot pursue true silence without rather quickly coming to a place of deep, dark doubt. Thomas Merton (1915-1968), a twentieth century monk, talks about this experience in a passage that deserves to be quoted in full:

> *The hermit, all day and all night, beats his head against a wall of doubt. That is his contemplation. Do not mistake my meaning. It is not a question of intellectual doubt, an analytical investigation of theological, philosophical, or some other truths. It is something else, a kind of unknowing of his own self, a kind of doubt which undermines his very reasons for existing and for doing what he does. It is this doubt which reduces him finally to silence, and in the silence which ceases to ask questions, he receives the only certitude he knows: the presence of God in the midst of uncertainty and nothingness, as the only reality....*
>
> *Beyond and in all this, he possesses his solitude, the riches of his emptiness his interior poverty: but of course, it is not a possession. It is an established fact. It is*

there. It is assured. In fact, it is inescapable. It is everything — his whole life. It contains God, surrounds him with God, plunges him in God.

Each of us probably desires and fears, in equal measure, being plunged into God. For there we must confront our deadliest sins and deepest doubts. But there, as Merton writes a few pages later, when we enter into the loneliness of the God who emptied himself on our behalf, "is a joy beyond human comment and appreciation. About such joy nothing can be said. Silence alone can worthily express it." We emerge from the dark night of the soul, if we have the patience and fortitude to endure it, stronger and more faithful.

It is often when we're swallowed up in God that we find our true selves. We discover our true identity, not as *do-ers*, but as *be-ers*. Our tasks in this life boil down to: "Be still, and know that I am God." Indeed, this is why many of us avoid silence and solitude: because our self-identities are bound up in our busy-ness. We're consumed with managing our lives, maintaining friendships, and loving our families. We may be doing all of this in an effort to love God, to do God's will (or is it to *earn* our salvation?!), but back in the recesses of our minds, we know that if we slow down long enough and become quiet long enough, all these things, tasks, events, and do-ings will recede in importance. Where then will we find identity? Although it's a frightening prospect to lose the things that give us meaning, the spiritual masters promise we'll find, in our silence, a meaning more profound than we could ever imagine.

Beyond this new self-identity, we find that silence and solitude also produce other spiritual fruits. As John Climacus tells us, "Intelligent silence is the mother of prayer, freedom from bondage, custodian of zeal, a guard on our thoughts, a watch on our enemies…a companion of stillness, the opponent of dogmatism, a growth of knowledge, a hand to shape contemplation, hidden progress, the secret journey upward." Ultimately, Richard Foster writes, "the fruit of solitude is increased sensitivity and compassion for others. There comes a new freedom to be with people. There is a new attentiveness to their needs, new responsiveness to their hurts." In other words, being quiet and being alone make us better, more spiritual, more Christ-centered human beings.

practice

Where I live, silence takes an enormous amount of discipline, and solitude takes even more. I'd like to do it at 5:30 a.m., but my kids often get up about then. I'd like to try silence, as many suggest, around Vespers time (late afternoon, before dinner), but my wife, Julie, calls that time with the kids "the arsenic hours"—you either want to give arsenic or take it. I'd like to engage in a time of silence at 9 p.m., reviewing the day, but that's the only time Julie gets to have adult conversation.

So, like many of the other practices, it's got to get on the calendar. I try to schedule one half-day of silence per month, a day-long silent retreat per year, a week-long silent retreat every five years, and—God willing—a 30-day Ignatian retreat before I die.

It takes a while to enter into true silence, and it takes effort to find solitude, but it can be found. Maybe someone in your church or a friend or neighbor has a lake home or a place in the mountains they'd let you borrow. There is surely a monastery or convent nearby that would let you make retreat there. Be creative. Take your tent to a state park and camp for a weekend. Bring a couple of the devotional classics commended in the back of this book. Try a couple practices, read a little, take a nap, walk in nature.

At first the silence can be scary, lonely, oppressive. But in time, it turns into joy and peace.

A final word

Kathleen Norris, award-winning author of *The Cloister Walk*, used to teach art to elementary students in the Dakotas. She worked hard to get these rambunctious little ones to settle down and be quiet so they could interact with art, so first she let them be loud and then she got them to be silent. Then she asked them to write about the noise and the silence:

What interests me most about my experiment is the way in which making silence liberated the imagination of so many children. Very few wrote with any originality about making noise. Most of their images were clichés such as "we sound like a herd of elephants." But silence was another matter: here, their images often had a depth and maturity that was unlike anything else they wrote. One boy came up with an image of silence being "as slow and silent as a tree," another wrote that "silence is me sleeping waiting to wake up. Silence is a tree spreading its branches to the sun." In a parochial school, one third grader's poem turned into a prayer: "Silence is spiders spinning their webs, it's like a silkworm making its silk. Lord, help me know when to be silent." And in a tiny town in western North Dakota a little girl offered a gem of spiritual wisdom

I find myself returning to when my life becomes too noisy and distractions overwhelm me: "Silence reminds me to take my soul with me wherever I go."

Henri Nouwen provides a nice epilogue that can probably be applied to many of us:

As ministers our greatest temptation is toward too many words. They weaken our faith and make us lukewarm. But silence is a sacred discipline, a guard of the Holy Spirit.

Taizé/Daily Office

There's something about the brothers who sit down the middle of the church during Taizé prayers. They're quite a magnetic presence- that is, it's hard to take your eyes off of them, especially because there's no real focal object at the front of the church-like a cross or an altar.

As I look at the brothers-maybe 100 of them are here-I can't help but wonder if they have chosen this life-long vocation because it's easier or harder. On the one hand, it obviously seems harder-they've given up their entire lives, everything they own, the possibility of marriage and family, and even their inheritances to serve Christ. On the other hand, by giving up all of those things and joining a community that demands total submission, all of their difficult choices have been taken away.

The same goes for the Daily Office. At Taizé, there are three prayer services per day: one before breakfast, one before lunch, and one after dinner-basically, Matins, Nones, and Compline. Silence is observed from the close of the service till dawn the next day. Sunday is a little different, with Eucharist after breakfast and 'common prayer' (vespers) before dinner.

So, in this case, the brothers have this ritualized routine-the bells ring, they head to prayer. It must be difficult, never getting to feel the grace of "skipping church," always being held accountable by a community. But they will never know the difficulties of trying to practice the Daily Office during their children's nap times or before running to a lunch meeting. So, it seems the ambivalent answer is correct: their life is not easier or harder than mine. Just different.

I've met a few people. Marcus is a 25-year-old Swede who's working for his second week in a row. He had been to Taizé several times as a participant, and has now come back to serve for two weeks. He seems to be having a good time; however, now that he's seen "behind the curtain," he says some of the mystery of Taizé spirituality has worn off.

Cole is a 29-year-old American from Boulder who is currently living and working in the Netherlands. He is a self-professed rich kid who drank, drugged, and sexed his way through college. He seems to despise the U.S., and plans to relinquish his citizenship and become a citizen of Holland.

Seven weeks ago, he had what he termed a nervous breakdown and, thanks to the Dutch national medical plan, he was sent for six weeks to a cushy hospital where he participated in groups and met with psychiatrists. One of the friends he made while he was there—a woman who helped him a lot—committed suicide while they were in the hospital. Since she helped Cole, he is determined to spend the rest of his life helping others.

He also met someone who had been to Taizé and who highly recommended the experience. So after his six weeks in the hospital, Cole headed to Taizé. He's already been here for four days, and he's planning to stay at least one more week, possibly in silence. He is enamored of modern philosophy and is fond of quoting Heidegger and Sartre.

What Cole likes about Taizé is the openness. He thinks that religious people in the States are very judgmental and parochial in their views. Here people are tolerant. Although the prayer services are clearly Christ-focused, there is no decree, no altar call, no measurement as to whether someone has "accepted Christ." "I may come out of this place believing in the resurrection," he told me, "or I may not. Either way, I'll be a lot closer to the kind of person I want to be and God wants me to be."

Lise is a 29-year-old from Amsterdam. I met her last night having a late night cup of tea at the Oyek with most of the other young people who were there. She is on her fourth trip to Taizé and today she began a week of silence. Although she grew up in Christian schools and a Christian home, she finds the churches in Holland to be very staid. She's thinking about visiting the Baptist church in Amsterdam when she gets back.

Lise's first trip to Taizé took place as part of a school trip when she was 17. That experience made a profound impression on her, thus her three visits since. Her response to the profundity of the Taizé worship and silence is not that she wants to become Catholic, but that she wants to find a community where faith is alive, unlike her parents' Reformed church.

When I asked her if she has continued to practice the Daily Office after she's gone home from Taizé, she responded like most American kids would after the fall retreat, a ski trip, or summer camp: "After Taizé, every time I say I'm going to continue to do things that keep that feeling going. But I can never keep it up."

chapter four
sacred Reading

Do not read to satisfy curiosity or to pass the time, but study such things as move your heart to devotion.

Thomas à Kempis

A friend of mine was struggling with his profession, or at least his current work environment. He'd been attracted to this company when he did some consulting work for them and was recruited to come on board full time. But after a couple years in the corporation, he began to see what an unhealthy and dysfunctional environment it was—the CEO was hostile and abusive, and the vast majority of the employees let him get away with it. But Peter was being paid well, they kept him busy, and he avoided the CEO as much as possible.

Then one day, he was in Las Vegas to train a group of employees to sell a line of products he had designed. Between the dysfunction of the organization and the general feeling of discomfort with much of what he saw in downtown

Vegas, Peter began to feel overwhelmed by grief. Heartsick, he rented a car and drove to Los Angeles to see some friends for the weekend. But instead of being his usual perky self, he holed up in a bedroom and lay on the bed, halfway between waking and sleeping. He drove back to Vegas Sunday night, dreading his Monday morning meeting with the CEO. In his hotel room that night, he opened his Bible and he decided to turn to the words of Jesus for help.

"I didn't even know where the Sermon on the Mount was," Peter told me, "But I looked around until I found it." That night, in the Embassy Suites in downtown Las Vegas, Peter read the fifth, sixth, and seventh chapters of St. Matthew's gospel over and over. The more he read, the more two sections stuck out to him: Jesus' admonition not to worry (Matthew 6:25-34) and Jesus' exhortation to ask, seek, and knock (Matthew 7:7-11). "Something in me broke," Peter said, "I went from feeling like a caged animal to having everything become slow and peaceful—I think I finally abandoned my life to Christ that night."

On Monday morning he called his wife and told her he was quitting his job. She wholeheartedly agreed with his decision, and Peter went into the meeting with his boss with the boldness of true faith.

This is *lectio divina*. *Lectio* (pronounced léx-ee-o) means reading, and *divina* (dih-vee-nah) means holy or sacred. Peter read the words of Christ with no agenda, no presuppositions (except despair of his current situation and faith that God speaks through the Bible). He came to the Bible naked, so to speak, and let himself be clothed by God's Word. He came neither as a Bible scholar nor a teacher getting ready for a lesson; he didn't have to stop every two verses and answer questions in a study guide. No, he read the Bible as a sacred object, as a living, dynamic revelation of God to *him*. And he read a complete section repeatedly and slowly, waiting for the revelation to be made known.

And indeed, God spoke to Peter that night.

History

Little did Peter know he was engaging in a method of reading Scripture that innumerable monks and nuns have used in their caves and cells, cloisters and sanctuaries since the earliest days of the church.

For the Israelites and the earliest Christians alike, the Psalter was their songbook. The 150 psalms that make up that book

were their primary prayers, meditations, and pleas to God. As
the New Testament was being compiled and immediately after,
many different "senses" of Scripture reading were developed and
articulated (see Theology section below), and one of them was the
meditative or devotional use of the Bible.

While the Desert Fathers and other early church leaders used
the Scripture for their devotions, it was St. Benedict (ca.480-
ca.550) who cemented the practice in Western monasticism. Born
in Nursia, Italy, Benedict went to school in Rome. Disgusted with
the sin of that city, he retreated to a village called Subaico in the
hills. Once there, his reputation spread, and small bands of followers began to live with him. He organized them into monasteries of 12 brothers, each led by a spiritual Father (Abbot). Around
529, many of them left Subaico and built a monastery at Monte
Cassino (you can still see it from the autostrada between Rome
and Naples), and around 540, Benedict wrote *The Rule of St. Benedict*. In *The Rule*, Benedict outlines life in a monastery, everything
from the seven worship services daily to how to do the dishes.

The three elements that guide the life of a Benedictine monk
are prayer, work, and lectio divina. The big difference between
Benedict and many of the other early monastics was that he had
little patience for solitaries, hermits, and all others who removed
themselves from community—for Benedict, the Rule had to
be lived out in community. And because of their dedication to
holy reading, both of Scripture and of the other great texts of
early Christianity, Benedictine monasteries were responsible for
safeguarding much of the great literature of the world during the
Dark Ages.

To understand the primacy that reading had in the life of a
Benedictine monastery, we might remember what we learned in
high school history class about the Dark Ages. Literacy was not
common—often only clerics and village royalty could read. Books
were scarce and exorbitantly expensive. Through Benedict's
description of a day in the monastery, it's clear that a significant
portion of the day is spent reading—mainly monks individually
reading books in a common room. Reading aloud is also a part of
each day, both at worship and at meals.

Lectio divina was articulated further by Guigo II (ca.1115
- ca.1198), the ninth prior of the Grand Chartreuse, a Carthu-
sian order in France. In his book *Scala Claustralium* (*The Ladder of
Monastics*), Guigo writes,

One day I was engaged in physical work with my hands and I began to think
about the spiritual tasks we humans have. While I was thinking, four spiritual
steps came to mind: reading (lectio), meditation (meditatio), prayer (oratio),
and contemplation (contemplatio). This is the ladder of monastics by which they
are lifted up from the earth into heaven. There are only a few distinct steps, but
the distance covered is beyond measure and belief since the lower part is fixed on
the earth and its top passes through the clouds to lay bare the secrets of heaven.

These four steps have been foundational in the practice of the
lectio divina ever since. Sacred reading is still practiced today in
Benedictine and similar monastic communities. Across Christianity it has become a popular method of approaching Scripture in
our information-saturated world.

Theology

As mentioned above, the Psalter was the song/prayer book of
Judaism and it continues to play that role today for both Jews
and Christians. But immediately after the writing and distribution
of the Gospels and epistles, the early Fathers had to go into a
defensive mode against those who were attacking the unity of the
Bible. Heretics like Marcion (d.c.160) questioned the inspiration
of the entire Old Testament and much of the New Testament.
Similar to the debates today between orthodox biblical scholars
and the Jesus Seminar, the Fathers had to develop scholarly,
credible means to defend the *literal* authenticity of Scripture.

At the time of the Reformation, Martin Luther and John Calvin advanced a Christocentric reading of Scripture that has heavily influenced Protestant interpretation ever since. And following
the scientific revolution of the Enlightenment, linguistic, histori-
cal-critical, text-critical, and redaction methods of interpretation,
developed primarily in nineteenth century Germany, have held
sway in some Protestant camps.

The early church fathers utilized another Jewish method of
reading the text, the *allegorical* method. An ancient Greek and
Hebrew tradition, allegory is when a deeper meaning is hidden
below the literal meaning of a passage—for example, reading
the lovers' story in the Song of Solomon as an allegory for the
relationship between Israel and God. In the Patristic period, the
allegorical method was very popular, sometimes leading to highly
dubious interpretations. The allegorical method fell into disrepute
in the wake of the Enlightenment as academics looked to more
intellectually credible interpretations of Scripture.

In addition to the literal or historical and allegorical means of interpreting Scripture, a third method is finding the *moral* meaning of a text. Using this method, the believer attempts to find application of the passage to her life or to her community of faith. Here one asks, "What is God saying to us about the world today?" This may be the most common mode of interpretation for preachers.

And finally, we come to a method of reading Scripture that inspires lectio divina: the *devotional* use of the Bible. One approaches the Bible devotionally believing that, because it is God's inspired Word, it's a living and active text, that has something to say to each individual believer. Few Christians would argue with reading the Bible devotionally; in fact, this is probably how most individual Christians approach Scripture.

Lectio divina assumes that, by entering deeply into the text of God's holy Word, God will be made known to us, speak to us, and shape our lives. Indeed, the apostle Paul teaches that God's Word is "inspired" and "profitable," assuming it is approachable by the average person. We need neither years of study nor thorough knowledge of both Testaments to profit from lectio. As God's unique revelation to humankind, Scripture is applicable to our lives and is the primary sourcebook for our devotion to God.

practice

Kathleen Norris has written of lectio divina: "It is not a method, but rather a type of free-form, serious play." To keep this in mind is of ultimate importance when developing a practice of sacred reading.

The initial preparation for practicing lectio is to purposefully shed the common methods most of us use in our everyday reading. The fact is, we read mostly for entertainment and information. Whether it be a novel, the newspaper, magazines, professional journals, or the Bible, we read almost exclusively for these two reasons. We need to approach the Bible differently for lectio. This is harder than it sounds, particularly for anyone trained in Bible study, either formally or informally.

First it means finding a Bible that's easily readable, without distracting notes and boxed-out "life applications." We should use a version that uses poetic form for the poetry and paragraph form for the prose. For this reason, many suggest the *New Jerusalem Bible* for accuracy of translation, not only in the words, but also in the rhythms and form of the Hebrew and Greek originals.

Eugene Peterson's paraphrase, *The Message*, is also excellent for lectio. Avoid using a Bible that has marks, underlined passages, or notes from past reading and study—they can distract you from what God is saying to you *today*.

Secondly, attend to the surroundings. Lectio divina requires quiet—even silence. Have enough light to read, but not so much to be distracting. Choose a time of day when you're wide awake, and neither too hungry nor too full to concentrate. Obviously, turn off the cell phone and any other external distractions. And carve out enough time to hear from God.

Thirdly, choose a text on which to meditate. Because it is God-inspired, the entirety of Scripture is able to be digested through lectio—but many parts are difficult to meditate on except for the most experienced reader. It's better for the beginner to choose from a more obvious source of devotion: a psalm, the epistles of John, Ecclesiastes, or any part of the Gospels.

Many people like to begin lectio with a prayer requesting—indeed, expecting—God's presence and direction. Others like to start with a kind of introduction, perhaps read the same section of the same psalm every day; Psalm 119 lends itself to this with its praise of God's Word:

> *I seek you with all my heart;*
> *do not let me stray from your commands.*
> *I have hidden your word in my heart*
> *that I might not sin against you.*
> *Praise be to you, O LORD;*
> *teach me your decrees.*
> *With my lips I recount*
> *all the laws that come from your mouth.*
> *I rejoice in following your statutes*
> *as one rejoices in great riches.*
> *I meditate on your precepts*
> *and consider your ways.*
> *I delight in your decrees;*
> *I will not neglect your word.*

From this point, we can step onto the rungs of Guigo II's ladder to guide us in lectio divina:

Lectio: Having chosen the passage on which you are going to meditate and situating yourself in a spot that's conducive to sacred reading, set about reading the section of Scripture slowly, repeatedly, and aloud if possible. Michael Casey calls this "active reading." He says, "We need to slow down, to savor what we read, and to allow the text to trigger memories and associations that reside below the threshold of awareness." This isn't the rapid reading of the morning paper or an e-mail; it's calm, deliberate, and gradual. I like to imagine what my temperament will be in heaven, sitting at God's feet, listening, and being instructed. I don't imagine I'll be shifting in my seat, my hand up to ask a question. I imagine I'll be content, calm, and listening hard for what God has to say to *me*. What I often find is that a certain word or phrase rises above the rest of the text and grabs a hold of me during my reading.

Meditatio (med-i-tá-tsee-o): Guigo calls this step the "interior intelligence" of the text. That is, what seem to be the values, the underlying assumptions and presumptions of this passage? As you attend to those deeper meanings, begin to meditate on the feelings and emotions that are conjured in your inner self. Different texts will evoke joy, sorrow, satisfaction, barrenness — and different individuals will experience different emotions in the same text.

Oratio (o-rá-tsee-o): Although the lectio is a prayer from beginning to end, Guigo emphasizes that on this rung in the ladder, one deliberately asks God for illumination. Again, this is an active step in lectio, conversing with God about the meaning of the emotions that are being experienced.

Contemplatio (con-tem-plá-tsee-o): The final step is the most difficult to describe and often the most difficult to achieve. True contemplation moves beyond words and intellect and into that "thin space" where time and eternity almost touch. It's in moments like these that some of the greatest saints in the history of the church have had a "mystical union" with Christ. That is not to say that contemplation is unavailable to you and me, just that it takes patience and practice. So don't get discouraged if your first attempts at contemplation seem unfulfilling. For me, it may be merely a moment of silence, peace, and rest in the midst of 10 minutes of struggle to quiet my mind, but that moment is a treasure beyond compare.

If this sounds like a lot of work, or a lot of time, consider what Guigo says of the four steps:

> *From what has been said we may gather that reading without meditation is dry. Meditation without reading is subject to error. Prayer without meditation*

is lukewarm. Meditation without prayer is fruitless. Prayer with devotion leads to contemplation whereas contemplation without prayer happens rarely or by a miracle.

One of my favorite aspects of the traditional lectio is that it lends itself to variations. Here are two I've found worth exploring:

Group Lectio: The practice of lectio can be an excellent experience for a group, and it's gaining popularity in churches and small groups around the world. Although the form can vary widely, it might look something like this: after an opening prayer, the passage is read two or three times, slowly and deliberately, and participants are asked to mull silently over the word or phrase that speaks to them. After a time for sharing that word with the others in the group, the passage is read two or three more times with a different voice (different gender, or two or three in unison). Again, in silence, participants reflect on the word or phrase that speaks to them, this time attending to the emotions or feelings that it conjures. Finally, after more time for sharing within small groups, the passage is read twice more, again in distinct voices, then a longer period of silence is kept to ask God why this word and this feeling have been provoked. A final and more lengthy time of sharing ends the session, with each person telling the small group what God is saying through the text.

Reading Non-Biblical Texts: St. Francis de Sales (1567-1622), a founder of the Modern Devotion movement, once wrote, "There is no more difference between the Gospel written and the life of a saint than between music written and music sung." Any Christian who has spent time reading some of the classics of Christian devotion (e.g., St. Augustine's Confessions, Thomas à Kempis's Imitation of Christ, St. John of the Cross' The Ladder of Divine Ascent) probably agrees with him. While all Christians hold the Bible as the inspired Word of God, and therefore the primary source of lectio divina, many of the great works of Christian faith can likewise lead us into deep devotion. If this kind of reading is new to you, experiment—you'll probably find an author or two in the Christian tradition with whom you particularly resonate.

Serious Bible study—working with the literal, allegorical, and moral senses of Scripture—will always be a part of following Jesus. But in approaching the Bible devotionally, we not only add to the angles by which we can come at God's Word, we have a method of reading that often results in this living Word giving us *life*. One way to keep track of the way God speaks to you in the lectio is to keep a *florilegium* (floor-i-lég-ium; literally, "a little book of flowers"), a book of the collected verses that have struck you over the years.

A final word

Guigo gets the last word on lectio:

> *Reading is an exterior exercise; meditation belongs to the inner intellect. Prayer operates at the level of desire. Contemplation transcends every sense. Reading is proper to beginners, meditation to proficients, prayer to those with devotion, and contemplation to the blessed.*

Reading Boiler Room

I'm manning the door at the Boiler Room in Reading, England. This is a place inspired by the 24/7 Prayer movement over here. A group of five churches in Reading, already committed to reaching youth in this city, banded together to open this place last October.

Reading was the site of a very powerful Abbey in the Middle Ages, but the Abbey was closed down after Henry VIII became a Protestant. Over the years, the buildings fell down, so only a couple walls remain. However, there seems to be a latent spirituality to this place. In fact, the major hang-out area for high school kids is in the square formerly occupied by the Abbey—I saw hundreds there today, it being Spring Break.

Ironically, many of the kids who hang out in that park are self-proclaimed Satanists. Malcolm, a staff member of the Boiler Room told me that they're not "really" Satanists as much as they are anti-Christians. They see Satan as the hero because he had the sense to flee the boredom and oppression of heaven, and they think of Jesus as a poser.

The Boiler Room is housed in a huge old pub with apartments upstairs. They welcome pilgrims like me with coffee, tea, and a place to stay. I was warmly greeted and Malcolm immediately signed me up for the unfilled prayer slots of the day: from midnight till 2 a.m.! Between people here in Reading and individuals throughout the world, they have had over 150 days of nonstop prayer. If no one signs up here or online, one of the staff members fills in the gaps.

I bought a paper and ate a late lunch (4 p.m.) at a pub, then I went up to the flat and slept for an hour. Around 7 p.m., a dozen people showed up for a prayer meeting for the Call, which is coming here this summer. Then I became the doorkeeper—this is a fairly rough neighborhood—squatters in the abandoned building next door sell and take drugs and regularly come by for food handouts. The BR keeps sandwiches on hand that are donated by restaurants at the end of the day.

A youth group showed up and met in one of the upstairs rooms—they're working through the Alpha Course.

I did a lot of Web surfing on different prayer resources and opened the door as people showed up for various meetings.

It's taken me a couple days to start to find the rhythm for the Daily Office. I'm a long way from it being part of my Rule of Life, but I'm starting to get the vibe for it. I can already tell that the point isn't for each time during the day to be an ecstatic experience, but to stop...to listen for God...to pray repentance.

chapter five
The Jesus prayer

Let all your thoughts be with the Most High, and direct your humble prayers unceasingly to Christ.

Thomas à Kempis

Sometime in the middle of the nineteenth century, a young man in his 20s set out on a quest. His wife had just died, and his right hand was withered from a childhood accident, making it uncommonly difficult for him to find work. He began to wander the countryside of his native Russia. He was embarking on a quest because he had recently heard in church the apostle Paul's exhortations to "pray without ceasing" and to "pray in the Spirit on all occasions," and he wanted to know if it was truly possible to maintain this kind of constant prayer.

Taking this biblical appeal more seriously than one might expect, he walked from town to town, seeking out priests, monks, and other wise elders who might help him answer this question. One day, while walking along a country road, a man in the clothing of a monk came to be walking alongside him. The young man posed to him the question of his quest: "Is unceasing prayer possible?" The old monk answered that indeed, it is possible to continually pray, and he invited the young man back to his monastery a few miles up the road to learn more about this.

As they approached the monastery, the old man explained that true ceaseless prayer comes in quieting the mind and making the mind one with the heart. As they entered the old man's cell, the young man was about to burst with curiosity: "Please, be gracious, Reverend Father, and explain the meaning of ceaseless mental prayer to me and show me how I can learn to practice it!"

The old hermit explained, "The ceaseless Jesus Prayer is a continuous, uninterrupted call on the holy name of Jesus Christ with the lips, mind, and heart; and in the awareness of His abiding presence it is a plea for His blessing in all undertakings, in all places, at all times, even in sleep. The words of the Prayer are: 'Lord Jesus Christ, have mercy on me.' Anyone who becomes accustomed to this Prayer will experience great comfort as well as the need to say it continuously. He will become accustomed to it to such a degree that he will not be able to do without it and eventually the Prayer will flow in him."

Then the old hermit handed the young pilgrim a book, the *Philokalia*, the collected works of the Desert Fathers, and pointed out to him the passages regarding the Jesus Prayer. The young man found a hut in which to live and he spent a week studying the selections from the *Philokalia*. He then went back to the old monk and asked him to become his *starets*, his spiritual director. The old man agreed and told the young man to go back to his hut and recite the Prayer 3,000 times per day. He also gave the young man a prayer rope with 100 knots to keep track of the number of recitations.

Although the first two days were challenging, the young man soon found the Prayer to be easy and delightful. A week later, he returned to his *starets* and told him these things. The old man told him to increase the repetitions to 6,000 per day. Within 10 days, the young pilgrim had grown so accustomed to the Prayer that he felt as though something was missing when he wasn't saying it, and this he told to his *starets* at their next meeting. "Do not waste any time," the *starets* replied, "but decide, with the help of God, to recite the Prayer 12,000 times a day. Rise earlier and retire later; stay alone, and every two weeks come to me for direction."

At first, the young man had great difficulty in following the hermit's direction. His tongue went numb and his jaw got tight. His thumb ached and his forearm swelled from working the rope. But as the days passed, the Prayer became the air that the pilgrim breathed; it woke him up in the morning, it overwhelmed him during the day, and he dreamed about it at night. Every recitation was pure joy, filling him with both emotional and physical light. He began to feel love for everyone he met, considering each his brother or sister.

Shortly thereafter, the young pilgrim's *starets* died and the pilgrim began once again to wander the Russian steppe country. He met many people along the way, many of whom he taught about the Prayer. On summer nights he slept under trees, and in winter he found for himself some kind of humble lodging. All the while, whether walking or resting, eating or sleeping, contemplating or working, he recited the Prayer, and the Prayer became one with him, reflecting his breath and his heartbeat.

The anonymous Russian pilgrim left us the story of his journeys and discoveries in the wonderful little book, *The Way of a Pilgrim*.

History

What the pilgrim happened upon in the 1850s has actually been a foundation of Eastern Christian spirituality since the fifth century. Following the aAge of the Apostles, those who knew and followed Jesus, was the Age of the Martyrs. The many who lost their lives to Roman persecution were looked to by early Christians as saints worthy of remembrance and veneration. In 312, the Emperor Constantine legalized and even promoted Christianity, making martyrs much less common. So Christians began to look to the first monks for wisdom. The tradition of monasticism (from the Greek, *monachus*, meaning "solitary person") began in the East where some men and women retreated from cities into the Egyptian and Syrian deserts. These people became known as the Desert Fathers and Mothers.

Their withdrawal from society was noteworthy, to be sure, but it was the teachings and writings from these desert dwellers that really began to attract some attention. Reports from the desert told of divine appearances, words from the Lord, and moments of mystical union with Christ. As these teachings circulated in both oral and written form, many city dwellers made pilgrimage to the desert to learn from the Fathers and Mothers.

In the West, however, the patristic period (that of the church fathers) was considered to be over in the seventh century. In the East, the witness of the Fathers and Mothers is considered ongoing. Although earlier Fathers wrote about contemplative prayer invoking Jesus' name, the first to mention the Jesus Prayer was Abba Philemon of the sixth century. Since Abba Philemon, dozens of Eastern contemplatives and mystics have written about the Prayer, making it the centerpiece of Eastern Christian spirituality.

The Way of a Pilgrim continued that trend into the modern era, endorsing the Jesus Prayer in a compelling and winsome, albeit anonymous, narrative. The pilgrim's story revitalized interest in the Prayer and in Eastern spirituality, and, partly as a result, the *Philokalia* was translated into English for the first time in the 1950s.

Theology

Beginning with the teaching of Origen (ca.185-254), Eastern theologians believed that body, mind, and spirit were so intimately intertwined that the soul could only truly commune with God if removed from all other distractions. Two emphases of the Eastern monastic movement have exerted influence since Origen and Gregory of Nyssa (ca.330-ca.395):

Asceticism (as-ké-ti-sizm) From the Greek word for training or exercise, asceticism follows from the teachings of Christ and Paul that Christians must deny themselves in order to follow Jesus. An ascetic, therefore, denies herself many of the pleasures common to a life lived in society, like marriage, sex, property, and generous portions of food. While the negative side of asceticism is voluntary forfeiture of these pleasures, the positive side is the opportunity to follow Christ exclusively, without the external hindrances these pleasures so often entail.

Hesychasm (héh-zee-kazm) From the Greek word for quietness, the hesychasts believed that if the mind could achieve true silence, then it could hear from God. Actually, Eastern theology has less to do with the individual receiving a word or divine instruction from the Lord, and more to do with mystical union with the Lord in his Divine Light. The way to do this, they taught, was to unite the mind and the heart in prayer, known as "the Prayer of the Heart." When this is truly accomplished, through quieting the mind, focusing it on the heart, and repetitively praying a simple phrase, God's Light will illumine the believer, particularly to the truths of Scripture.

Although these are strange Greek words, I mention them because they are so unfamiliar to many of us yet so essential to understanding monastic spirituality. In fact, at first blush we may completely disagree with both of these ideas — doesn't God desire us to be in but not of the world? What good are monks anyway? Isn't it just escapism to run off to the desert in order to commune with God?

Good questions all. But many of us know how powerful retreats are. Some of the best times with God take place *away* from the distractions of work and home. And we ourselves are fueled when we spend a time apart from friends, work, even family, to reconnect with God for a time. What these Desert Fathers and Mothers did was to extend the retreat over the course of 30 or 40 years in some cases, all the while sending correspondence back to the "real world" — though one might argue that the union with Christ they experienced is actually the *most* real world.

The result of a retreat to the desert and what's variously called the Prayer of the Heart, mental prayer, or self-activating prayer, according to Gregory of Sinai (d.1360), is gradient:

> *To some there comes the spirit of fear, rending the mountains of passions and breaking in pieces on the rocks — hardened hearts — such fear that the flesh seems to be pierced by nails and numbed as in death. Others quake, being filled with joy — what the fathers called the leaping of joy. In yet others, preeminently in those who have achieved success in prayer, God produces a subtle and serene glow of light when Christ comes to dwell in the heart and to shine mysteriously in the spirit.*

Ultimately, some of the desert dwellers experienced Christ's light in an even more powerful and dramatic way, an experience that was often compared to the disciples' vision of Jesus, Moses, and Elijah on the Mount of Transfiguration.

Of course, the Prayer itself is strongly rooted in the Gospels, an amalgam of many who called out to Jesus, including blind Bartimaeus by the side of the road who shouted, "Jesus, son of David, have mercy on me," and the tax collector in Jesus' parable who beat his breast and cried out, "God, have mercy on me, a sinner." The cry for mercy, for God's unrelenting steadfast love, is a constant of Scripture, Old and New Testaments alike. The need for God's mercy seems obvious, upon reflection, but, Frederica Mathewes-Green writes:

The problem is not in God's willingness to have mercy, but in our forgetting that we need it. We keep lapsing into ideas of self-sufficiency, or get impressed with our niceness, and so we lose our humility. Asking for mercy reminds us that we are still poor and needy, and fall short of the glory of God. Those who do not ask do not receive, because they don't know their own need.

To cry out for mercy as a helpless sinner seems foreign to modern sensibilities, even to modern Christianity. All the more reason for us to make a practice of doing it.

practice

There is some variation in the actual form of the Prayer. The simple formulation, "Christ, have mercy on me," echoes the ancient cry of the church, *"Kurie eleison, Christe eleison, Kurie eleison* ('Lord, have mercy; Christ, have mercy; Lord, have mercy')." The fuller text of the Prayer combines the Scripture passages quoted above: *"Lord Jesus Christ, Son of God, have mercy on me, a sinner."*

While the final self-referential tag, "a sinner," seems like a harsh conclusion, it is, of course, the truth. Many modern recitations of the Prayer omit this ending, but I always use it in my own practice. It stings me and awakens me to my own weakness. It also makes the Prayer a loop, for as I conclude by considering my own sinfulness, I'm compelled to once again call upon God's mercy for my life. In this way, when practiced rhythmically, the Prayer has no beginning and no end.

The *Philokalia* is full of hundreds of pages of advice about practicing the Jesus Prayer. Among them are the instructions left by fourteenth century monks Callistus and Ignatius, who were said to have left behind "full and perfect knowledge of the Jesus Prayer." They recommend that a person be firstly, "earnest and undistracted," and in a place of absolute silence — silence being the most important thing to guard, and the most difficult for us to find in a modern world. For me this often means getting up early in the morning before the family rises — I find the world to be quietest at about 4 a.m.

Callistus and Ignatius also recommend a "dimly lit room." While the Prayer can later be practiced outside in nature, in a public place, or even while driving, at first it's necessary to sequester oneself from all visual distractions as well. This way whether the eyes are open or shut, concentration can be focused solely on the Prayer.

Now that the external setting is taken care of, the most important aspect of preparation for the Prayer can take place. With great concentration, one can cause "the mind to descend into the heart with the breath." At first, this was a concept as foreign to me as it may be to you. However, with some practice, this method becomes a means of guarding the mind from diversions. In fact, many of the Fathers recommend that one bows the head and fixes the eyes on the place of the heart in order to facilitate this concentration.

The "place of the heart" is obviously the focus of the Prayer of the Heart. It's difficult for us to imagine the heart without thinking of pumps, paddles, hospitals, and bypasses. But remember:

In ancient times, before the interior of the body was charted, emotions were ascribed to sites throughout the torso: heart, kidneys, bowels, and womb. The spiritual heart is not the same as that general region of feeling or compassion. Nor is it merely the fleshy pump that beats in our chests. This heart is the spiritual center of a person's entire being.

So, seated comfortably in a dimly lit room with the head bowed, attend to your breathing, and then begin the prayer in rhythm with your breathing. Breathe in: "Lord Jesus Christ, Son of God"; breathe out: "have mercy on me, a sinner." Guarding the mind against all distractions, the pray-er focuses during every repetition on the meaning of the words, praying them from the heart and in the heart.

Since clocks were not a reality when the Prayer was first practiced, instead of designating an amount of time to pray, a number of repetitions was determined ahead of time. The pilgrim started at 3,000 repetitions per day—if the normal person takes between 12 and 15 breaths per minute, this takes between three and four hours. When the pilgrim got to 12,000 repetitions, it was taking him between 11 and 14 hours. That's probably out of reach for you and me, but 100 or 500 prayers is a valuable and achievable practice.

In order to keep track of my repetitions, I use a prayer rope (called a *chockti* in Slavonic and a *komvoschinon* in Greek). Most are made in monasteries on Mt. Athos in Greece with 100 knots, each knot tied with nine crosses (though they also come with 33, 50, and 1,000 knots). After every 25 knots is a bead, at which the Lord's Prayer can be recited, and at the end I say the Apostles'

Creed. Prayer ropes can be purchased online (see the Resources section at the end of this book) and at many Orthodox churches.

A final word

Although I'll give the final word to Callistus and Ignatius, I do want to note first that the Jesus Prayer has become very significant to me, maybe more than any other practice I've investigated, and it's an important part of my Rule of Life. Now, here are Fathers Callistus and Ignatius:

> *When you will be worthy of the gift of ceaseless prayer in the heart, then, according to Isaac of Syria, you will have reached the summit of all virtues and become a dwelling place of the Holy Spirit; then the prayer will not cease, whether you sit, walk, eat, drink, or do anything else. Even in deep sleep, prayer will be active in you without any effort, for even when it is externally silent, it continues secretly to act within.*

Daily Office/Pilgrimage

I'm in a Starbucks in the shadow of Westminster Abbey. I woke this morning at 6:30 to begin morning prayers and the routine of the daily office. What freedom! What a difference from a "Quiet Time." The structure, the purpose(fulness), the direction. It seems that the office, and, by extenuation, the whole day, is on a line. It's like I'm actually "going somewhere" with my day.

I started reading *The Illumined Heart* this morning, and Frederica Mathewes-Green has such a way of saying with simplicity, beauty, and poetic prose the universal desire of the human heart.

How poignant to read that in every person, "there remains a melancholy awareness that each of us is still fundamentally alone, encapsulated in skin like a spaceman," as I sat alone in a B&B in London. I am truly alone here, separate from Julie and the kids, apart from my friends and my church. There is freedom in that, for good and ill, but there's also loneliness.

chapter six
centering prayer

Choose a suitable time for reflection and frequently consider the loving-kindness of God.

Thomas à Kempis

In 1989, the unthinkable happened to Dick and Carolyn: their 27-year-old son died in a car accident. It has been said that the most intense pain that a human being can experience is the death of a child. Dick and Carolyn wholeheartedly agree with this statement. They were plunged into deep darkness, not knowing where to turn for comfort. They felt as though they could not go on with life — they felt like lost souls, as though they had lost meaning in their lives.

As with most churches, theirs encouraged them to get into a support group, to talk it out in therapy, and to be faithful participants in worship. All these things helped, but the words started to ring hollow — and it was a lot of words, between support groups, therapists, sermons, and wordy prayers. Still, deep within them both was an almost indescribable pain, a deep, piercing pain that kept them up at night and brought them to tears at inopportune moments.

And then, a while after their son's death, they read *Healing into Life and Death* by Stephen Levine. Prompted by this book, Dick and Carolyn decided to go on a retreat and try Centering Prayer. Although they had never heard of it before, these two grieving parents were open to just about anything that might assuage their pain. They went to the Villa Maria Retreat Center in southern Minnesota and learned this ancient/modern art from the Ursuline nuns there.

"After three years of daily Centering Prayer, the pain was gone," Dick told me. "I still miss my son, but the pain, loss, and grief that had paralyzed me for three years miraculously lifted. And the same thing happened for Carolyn."

Dick and Carolyn continue to practice Centering Prayer every day. It's the axis on which their spiritual lives pivot. And I think, if you met them, you would agree with me that they are two of the most joyous and peaceful persons you've ever met.

History

Like the Jesus Prayer, Centering Prayer grew out of the reflections and writings of the Desert Fathers. John Cassian (ca.360-ca.430) came from the West and made a pilgrimage to the desert to learn the ways of contemplative prayer. After almost 20 years in the desert, Cassian was appointed a deacon in Constantinople, and by 415 he had returned to France where he established two monasteries, one for men and one for women. Cassian was deeply influenced by his time in the desert, and he wrote his book *The Conferences* about his conversations with the Desert Fathers to acquaint western Christians with their teachings.

Cassian writes about one conference he had with Abba Isaac who taught him the essence of "true prayer." "To maintain an unceasing recollection of God, this formula must be ever before you," Abba Isaac told Cassian. "The formula is this: 'O God, come to my assistance; O Lord, make haste to help me.'" The result, Isaac said, is that, "by God's light the mind mounts to the manifold knowledge of God, and thereafter feeds on mysteries loftier and more sacred…like a spark leaping up from a fire, the mind is rapt upward, and, destitute of the aid of senses or of anything visible or material, pours out its prayers to God."

Cassian's approach to contemplative prayer was the primary monastic practice for 10 centuries in the West, influencing Benedict, among others. However, during the Scholastic period (twelfth to fifteenth centuries), theologians like Thomas Aquinas brought the West out of the Dark Ages by recovering the works of Aristotle and other ancient thinkers. As a result, intellectual theology became the "Queen of the Sciences," and contemplative spirituality was demoted to a remnant of the superstitious past.

In the fourteenth century, just as the form of the Jesus Prayer was becoming concrete in the East, a mystic in England who remained anonymous by choice, wrote the first spiritual classic in our language, *The Cloud of Unknowing*. Rebelling against the intellectual currents of the day, the author of *The Cloud of Unknowing* urges a return to "Prayer of the Heart." In 75 admonitions to his spiritual disciple, the author teaches a method of prayer in which the pray-er ascends above the "cloud of forgetting" where all creatures and all thoughts dwell, and rises toward the "cloud of unknowing" in which God dwells. Of course, these aren't physical locales, but existential realities, bringing the contemplative into the "mystical silence" between the two clouds.

The basic method promoted in *The Cloud* is to move beyond thinking into a place of utter stillness with the Lord:

> *Here is what you are to do: lift your heart up to the Lord, with a gentle stirring of love desiring him for his own sake and not for his gifts. Center all your attention and desire on him and let this be the sole concern of your mind and heart. Do all in your power to forget everything else, keeping your thoughts and desires free from involvement with any of God's creatures or their affairs in general or in particular. Perhaps this will seem like an irresponsible attitude, but I tell you, let them all be; pay no attention to them.*

Unlike the Jesus Prayer, a repetitive prayer is not used. The pray-er is encouraged to choose a simple, monosyllabic word, like "love" or "God." When the mind is distracted, this word is used to bring the mind back to focus on God: "Should some thought go on annoying you demanding to know what you are doing, answer with this one word alone." This is true mental calm, dwelling with God who came to the Old Testament prophet Elijah in the "sheer silence." The result of practiced contemplation, promises the author, is an experience of the fullness of God's love.

The Cloud was widely read and much loved by English speakers of its day, but the intellectual emphasis of Scholasticism ultimate-

ly overwhelmed mystical and spiritual writings in influence. In
the latter half of the twentieth century, however, Christians were
looking for sources of contemplation, meditation, and mysticism.
As the world became more connected and "grew smaller," Eastern
traditions infiltrated the West. In the 1960s and 1970s, Yoga (a
Hindu practice), Zen Buddhism, Transcendental Meditation, and
other forms of Eastern meditation influenced thousands of Ameri-
cans. In response, some Trappist monks looked to Cassian and
The Cloud, as well as to St. Theresa of Ávila and St. John of the
Cross, for guidance. They distilled these teachings into a Chris-
tian method of contemplative prayer that has become known as
Centering Prayer.

Theology

We have already noted the theological and spiritual influences of
the East on John Cassian. Cassian opposed the radical grace of
Augustine, the dominant Christian theologian of his (or any) day.
Whereas Augustine argued that humans are totally dependent on
God's grace for salvation, Cassian held that humans participate
by moving towards God—choosing him—and cooperate as
God's grace kicks in. This idea is seen in Cassian's practice of
prayer: the believer must first achieve a state of silence and
contemplation, and then God works in the believer's heart.
While Cassian's theology wouldn't be considered particularly
unorthodox by many today, in his day it wasn't politically wise
to oppose Augustine, and so Cassian's writings were originally
influential only in France.

Another theological charge that has been leveled against *The
Cloud* is Quietism. In the seventeenth century, some in France
took the writings of St. Theresa of Ávila, who promoted a "prayer
of quiet," to extremes. Quietists taught the pray-er to become
utterly passive, to the point of annihilating the will. Any thought,
even of Christ or the cross or one's own salvation, was rejected.
This led to great moral laxity, since outward behaviors had no influence on the inner quiet of the person. For good reason, Quietism was condemned in 1687 and died out shortly thereafter.

Centering Prayer, however, isn't quietistic. As opposed to annihilating the will, the pray-er moves into God's presence and rests
there. The human will isn't destroyed; to the contrary, it finds
peace in its true home. The contemplative person first acknowl-
edges the love that God has for creation and then quiets the mind
in order to rest in, center on, and contemplate that love.

In fact, the author of *The Cloud* goes to great lengths to relate the Christ-centeredness of the Prayer. For several chapters he reflects on the story from Luke's Gospel in which Martha is busy preparing a meal for Jesus while Mary sits quietly at his feet. While Martha goes about the necessary tasks of the "active life," Mary exemplifies the "contemplative life." Mary is quite unconcerned with the activity around her, content instead to sit at Jesus' feet and rest in his presence. Regarding Martha's work, Mary "forgot all of this and was totally absorbed in the highest wisdom of God concealed in the obscurity of his humanity...Mary turned to Jesus with all the love of her heart...She sat there in perfect stillness with her heart's secret, joyous love intent upon that *cloud of unknowing* between her and her God."

The Cloud's author imagines that Mary isn't reflecting on Jesus' body or voice or words, but has moved beyond images and senses to center on Jesus the Christ, her Christ. She is basking in his love for her. This makes Centering Prayer different from Ignatian meditation, for instance, where the pray-er places him or herself in the biblical narrative and attends to the sights and sounds and smells of the story.

M. Basil Pennington, one of the Trappist monks who has developed the modern practice of Centering Prayer, writes, "Centering Prayer is an opening, a response, a putting aside of all the debris that stands in the way of our being totally present to the present Lord, so that he can be present to us. It is a laying aside of thoughts, so that the heart can attend immediately to him." This method neither replaces nor subjugates other forms of prayer, but in fact enhances them—prayers of praise, petition, intercession, and the like then spring from gratitude, from a deep experience of God's love.

practice

It might seem that the only instruction necessary for Centering Prayer is "Be Quiet." But indeed there is a method to the practice. Basil Pennington describes the necessity thus:

> *The method of Centering Prayer is like a trellis. It is of the very nature of a climbing rose to reach up toward the sun and blossom forth. But without a trellis it keeps falling back on itself, and soon we have a large knotted mass that does not rise very high and gives birth to very few blooms. But if the climbing rose is given the support of a trellis, it can reach up and up toward*

the sun — the Sun of Justice and Life — and bear an ever greater abundance
of blossoms.

The work of Pennington and other Trappist monks of St.
Joseph's Abbey in Spencer, Massachusetts, has been to compose
this method. While the number of steps varies between authors,
the basic formulation is this:

1. As you sit comfortably with your eyes closed, let yourself
   settle down. Let go of all the thoughts, tensions, and sen-
   sations you may feel and begin to rest in the love of God
   who dwells within.
2. Effortlessly, choose a word, the symbol of your intention
   to surrender to God's presence, and let the word be gently present within you. The word should be one syllable,
   if possible, and should communicate God's love to you.
3. When you become aware of thoughts or as internal sen-
   sations arise, take this as your signal to gently return to
   the word, the symbol of your intention to let go and rest
   in God's presence.
4. If thoughts subside and you find yourself restfully aware,
   simply let go even of the word. Just be in that stillness. When thoughts begin to stir again, gently return
   to the word. Use the one word as your only response to
   thoughts, questions, or anxieties that arise in your mind.
5. At the end of your prayer time (20 minutes in the morning and evening is a good balance), take a couple of minutes to come out of the silence — even if you don't feel you
   need it. Many people find this a perfect time to internally
   express to God their thanks and to pray for others in
   need of God's grace. Slowly reciting the Lord's Prayer is
   another gentle way to come out of the prayer.

Centering Prayer takes time. In our noisy world it's extremely
difficult to quiet down at all — in fact, it's even difficult to find a
place that's quiet for 20 minutes. So, of course, Centering Prayer
takes discipline: first the discipline to find the time and place for
it, and then the mental discipline not to follow the rabbit holes
that our active minds so often take us down.

The result of Centering Prayer is *not* a word from the Lord or
any sort of divine revelation. Experts in the Prayer emphasize
that the pray-er should have no goal in mind for the practice. In
fact, the Prayer comes to fruition not in the minutes it is practiced, but throughout the day and throughout life. And, as it

should be, that *fruit*ion is most often the fruit of the Spirit: love, joy, peace, patience, kindness, generosity, faithfulness, gentleness, and self-control.

For instance, I know a dad who, every morning before work, lights a candle for each of his children and sits in silence before God. When the children come down for breakfast, they see the burned candle and know their dad has prayed for them and has been in God's presence. He notes how much more peace he feels during the day and how much less he worries about the safety and welfare of his children. He honestly feels that their futures are in God's hands.

Now, as his children are getting older, they occasionally join their dad in his silent meditation. He doesn't really explain what he's doing, and they don't really need an explanation. Even young children, when it's modeled for them, can be quiet in God's presence.

Basil Pennington agrees:

> *I should think that this kind of prayer could not only be attractive to young people but greatly help them in working through their identity struggles. Adolescents often like to go off by themselves to "get in touch" and just kind of "be with" things. To give them a little method to do this and to give them a sense of God's presence, that in some way Jesus is with them and they have in him a loving and caring friend, can be a priceless gift.*

A final word

From *The Cloud of Unknowing*:

> *There are some who believe that contemplation is so difficult and so terrible an experience that no one may reach it without great struggle and then only relish it rarely in those moments of ecstasy called ravishing. Let me answer these folk as best I can.*

> *The truth is that God, in his wisdom, determines the course and the character of each one's contemplative journey according to the talents and gifts he has been given. It is true that some people do not reach contemplation without long and arduous spiritual toil and even then only now and again know its perfection in the delight of ecstasy called ravishing. Yet, there are others so spiritually refined by grace and so intimate with God in prayer that they seem to possess and experience the perfection of this work almost as they like, even in the midst of their ordinary daily routine, whether sitting, standing, walking, or kneeling. They manage to retain full control and use of their physical and spiritual faculties at all times.*

Sabbath

I'm on the plane to London. This morning at church was a bittersweet experience. So many people had read my letter to the congregation explaining my sabbatical and they wished me well, said I'd be in their prayers, etc. But it was very sad to say goodbye.

It was surprising how many times I was tempted to say, "Oh, that's alright, you can call me." I told a couple of people, "You can contact me, but not as a pastor; only as a friend." They both responded: "When have I ever contacted you as a pastor?"

I have definitely felt anxiety as this trip and this sabbatical have approached: How much will I miss my family while I travel? Am I really ready/worthy to write a book on spirituality? Will I find out things about myself that I don't want to know?

chapter seven
meditation

If you avoid unnecessary talk and aimless visits,
listening to news and gossip, you will find plenty of time
to spend in meditation on holy things.

Thomas à Kempis

Mike King is a good friend of mine; he lives in Kansas City and runs a Christian non-profit organization:

Looking back, it was a major crossroad in my life. I needed to get away and hear from God. During my week away with Jesus, I focused on this passage:

The next day John was there again with two of his disciples. When he saw Jesus passing by, he said, "Look, the Lamb of God!"

When the two disciples heard him say this, they followed Jesus. Turning around, Jesus saw them following and asked, "What do you want?"

They said, "Rabbi" (which means Teacher), "where are you staying?"

"Come," he replied, "and you will see."

So they went and saw where he was staying, and spent that day with him.

I read this text practicing lectio divina several times a day. I used phrases from it for Centering Prayer. I meditated, contemplated, and prayed with this amazing text. Four days into my retreat I climbed up the side of a mountain, rolled out a blanket, and used the Ignatian prayer exercise of imaginative prayer to interact with the words.

I had determined to imagine and pray through this text in real time. I didn't have to spend a lot of time imagining the geography, the smells, the sounds, because I have been to Israel 20 times so I know, approximately, where this event took place. I know what the Jordan River looks like near the Dead Sea, close to Jericho. I know what the weather is like, how thick the vegetation is near the meandering banks of the Jordan River. I was able to fixate on what may of happened when Jesus came over the bank and headed toward John the Baptist and his delegation.

I imagined myself sitting around John's breakfast fire with his disciples, listening as his disciples began to discuss the plans for another day of baptizing. I imagined the personalities of these people who would follow the unconventional "baptizer" into this desolate area. And then, Jesus came through the thick vegetation over the bank toward John's camp next to the Jordan River. John stopped mid-sentence and said, "Look, the Lamb of God!" I saw John and his cousin Jesus embrace.

Jesus and the few who were with him joined us around the fire. I imagined what it would have been like to hear stories of Jesus and John's boyhood visits to each other's families. I heard laughter along with serious discussions of God and his coming kingdom. Wow, what it would have been like to hang out with Jesus and John like this!

And then Jesus abruptly rose to leave. They said their goodbyes and Jesus and his few followers left. The two disciples of John followed Jesus and I imagined myself right behind them, going along to see what would happen. We hit a trail through the thicket heading into the desert. As we came into a clearing Jesus turned around, seeing the two disciples of John following him. What happened next is just as real to me as if I were actually there in the text.

I have shared this experience about a dozen and a half times, never without tears because of how deeply this shaped me. Even writing this now is very emotional.

When Jesus turned around, the two disciples of John whom I was following parted like the Red Sea and Jesus came right up to me, face to face. Jesus looked past my eyes into my heart and soul:

"Mike, what do you want?"

I fell at the feet of Jesus and wept, pouring my heart out, praying, confessing, and in the end my answer was the same as John's disciples. "Where are you staying? Because that is right where I want to be. I want you Jesus. I want to remain with you. To go where you go, to learn from you, to love you, to be with you."

For one year after that experience I meditated every day on this text. I have often used imaginative prayer since that experience. Many times the Holy Spirit has met me and spoken to me, though never with the intensity I experienced God that day on the side of a mountain. But that day changed me profoundly and is something I will have for the rest of my life, for Jesus said, "Come, and you will see…"

History

In his opening words to Joshua after Moses' death, the Lord tells the new leader to meditate on God's Word day and night. The Psalmist gives more than a dozen admonitions for us to meditate. The word itself is absent from the New Testament, although the King James Version does translate 1 Timothy 4:15, "Meditate upon these things; give thyself wholly to them; that thy profiting may appear to all."

The modern conception of meditation, however, doesn't have a long history—that is, meditation as considered distinct from contemplative prayer. As a method of inner quieting, Judeo-Christian meditation goes back as far as Joshua and Psalm 46, "Be still and know…" As a Christian practice, it's inextricably bound up with the previous three practices: silence, the Jesus Prayer, and Centering Prayer, as well as with the next practice, the Ignatian Examen.

Further, it's linked with the recent popularity in the West of Eastern religions, resulting in books with such titles as *Christian Zen* and *Christian Yoga*. While this makes some Christians nervous, others revel in the fact that God is revealed in all truth, no

matter the religion of origin. But before delving into these controversial waters, we must talk terminology and distinguish the two
types of Christian meditation.

There is some debate within Christian circles about the terms
meditation and *contemplation*. While Protestant Christians use
the term *contemplation* fairly loosely, referring to quieter types
of prayer, Roman Catholics have a more strict definition of the
word. To them, *contemplation* means true inner silence, which has
been achieved in perfection by only a few of the great saints of
the church; whereas meditation has content, contemplation does
not. While this book sticks with the Protestant understanding of
the word, I acknowledge that most Catholics wouldn't use the
word this way.

That being said, the more ancient type of meditation, and at
times the more closely linked with Hinduism and Buddhism, is
apophatic or *nondiscursive* meditation. In this method of meditation,
the mind is emptied, much like Centering Prayer. In some forms
of the practice, no images or words are used, resulting in a total
emptying, without even the "word" used in Centering Prayer.
This type of meditation is an outgrowth of the Desert Fathers'
writings, as well as John Cassian's *Ladder of Divine Ascent*, the writings of St. John of the Cross, and *The Cloud of Unknowing*.

At the end of the twentieth century, Benedictine monk John
Main pioneered a Christian form of meditation that was influenced by his study with a Hindu master. He taught a form of
meditation using the word *maranatha* (Aramaic for "Come, Lord")
as a mantra. Sitting cross-legged, the meditator chants (either
aloud or silently) "ma-ra-na-tha" for 20 minutes twice daily. The
teachings of Brother Main and others became so popular that
the Vatican's Congregation for the Doctrine of the Faith issued a
letter to all Catholic bishops in 1989, entitled "Some Aspects of
Christian Meditation" to guide the bishops in their leadership of
churches that were using meditation.

The other type of Christian meditation is known as *discursive* or
guided meditation. This method uses words and images to usher
the individual or a group into God's presence. Ignatius of Loyola
is the most influential source of discursive meditation. In the *Spiritual Exercises*, Ignatius teaches his readers to use their five senses
to enter into a biblical scene. Once there, the meditator listens to
the conversations taking place, smells the food, touches Christ's
robe, and tastes the wine. *Discursive* means "conversational", and
Ignatius concludes these types of exercises by having the medita-

tor imagine a conversation with Christ in the midst of the biblical scene—for instance, on the road to Emmaus.

Discursive meditation hasn't been used much outside of the Ignatian Exercises until recently. Protestants, influenced by Martin Luther's doctrine of *sola scriptura* (meaning "Scripture alone"), have shied away from methods that interject anything into the biblical narrative. However, guided meditation has been used more recently across confessional lines, even to help some find healing from eating disorders, sexual sin, and addictions.

Apophatic meditation has been altogether more controversial. Because Buddhist and Hindu meditation extol a similar self-emptying, many Christians are uncomfortable with it. And indeed, many of the proponents of apophatic meditation have admittedly been influenced by Eastern religions. But whereas the goal of Buddhist meditation is to completely empty the self, the Christian purpose for this emptying is to be filled with the love of God. As official Roman Catholic teaching says:

> *Therefore, one has to interpret correctly the teaching of those masters who recommend "emptying" the spirit of all sensible representations and of every concept, while remaining lovingly attentive to God. In this way, the person praying creates an empty space which can then be filled by the richness of God. However, the emptiness which God requires is that of the renunciation of personal selfishness, not necessarily that of the renunciation of those created things which he has given us and among which he has placed us. There is no doubt that in prayer one should concentrate entirely on God and as far as possible exclude the things of this world which bind us to our selfishness. On this topic St. Augustine is an excellent teacher: if you want to find God, he says, abandon the exterior world and re-enter into yourself. However, he continues, do not remain in yourself, but go beyond yourself because you are not God; he is deeper and greater than you.*

It seems likely that as our world becomes "smaller," as we live in neighborhoods and apartments next to Hindus and Buddhists, and as more people become interested in yoga and transcendental meditation, Christian meditation will gain popularity, too. Still, if recent history is any indication, more controversy may come before the church finds an acceptable practice of meditation.

Theology

"Christian meditation can be nothing but loving, reflective, obedient contemplation of him who is God's self-expression. He is the very explanation of God and his teaching to us." With this statement, theologian Hans Urs von Balthasar reminds us that the focus of Christian meditation must be Jesus Christ.

The great articulator of the Christ-centered faith was the apostle Paul, who established the doctrine of the real presence of the risen Christ in the heart of the believer. Confession of the lips and belief in the heart was his standard for salvation; and meditation, when rightly practiced, is a focusing of the heart on Christ.

I say, "when rightly practiced" because there are numerous examples of a distortion of Christian meditation in the history of the church. But the orthodoxy of Christian meditation can be tested, for, when rightly practiced, it always leads to the same result: "Contemplative Christian prayer always leads to love of neighbor, to action, and to the acceptance of trials, and precisely because of this it draws one close to God." Love of God and love of neighbor is the inevitable result of true Christian meditation, whether discursive or apophatic.

In addition to being Christ-centered, Christian meditation depends upon a theology of the Holy Spirit. As von Balthasar reminds us, "The vistas of God's Word unfold to the meditating Christian solely through the gift of the Divine Spirit." Indeed, the Christian meditator knows that any result of meditation, whether it be "divinization" (mystic union with Christ) or "the dark night of the soul," is a gift of the Holy Spirit. And here's another place where the Christian differs from her Hindu and Buddhist peers: whereas their meditation is thoroughly human, in origin and result, Christian meditation is ultimately guided by God.

Finally, we should look at two Latin words. In Latin, the word for contemplation is *theoria* and the word for conversion is *praxis*. While *theoria* is related to theory and ideas, *praxis* is related to practical ideas and practice. In the theology of meditation, these two are inseparable — there is no contemplation without a resulting conversion. That is, we don't contemplate merely as a sign of self-sacrifice to God. We meditate in order to be changed, to be converted from old habits and sins and vices. Meditation, though it's silent and still, challenges us in rigorous ways.

practice

Apophatic meditation requires silence. Like the Jesus Prayer and Centering Prayer, the required self-emptying demands that the meditator finds a place of true quiet where distractions will be at a minimum. Of course, mental distractions will still come, but over time and practice, these too can be overcome.

Some, like John Main, recommend a mantra: "Maranatha" or "Come, Lord Jesus," or something of the sort. A seated posture is recommended, either in a chair with both feet firmly on the ground or cross-legged on the floor. The goal of apophatic meditation is inner quiet, which leads to peace. As well as abiding in heaven and over the earth, God also dwells within the believer. To be utterly quiet and go within gives the believer a much better chance to touch God within, and then peace, compassion, and an increased ability to love result.

Discursive meditation often takes place in a group. Relative quiet is best, but the absolute quiet of apophatic meditation isn't required. A leader guides the group through a set of images or through a biblical story, pausing to allow the participants to imagine the scene. At the end of the group exercise, participants are often given the opportunity to reflect on their experience, sometimes aloud with other group members, in their journals, or even by painting or drawing the scene they imagined.

I distinctly remember sitting under a tree at church camp in northern Minnesota. It was the summer before my sophomore year in high school, and I was about to embark on the adventure of being a camp counselor for the first time. Paul, the camp director, sat all of the counselors under this tree; he asked us to be comfortable but not lie down. After a couple minutes of silence, he started to speak very slowly and gently:

Imagine yourself walking down a road. It's the path of your life. Imagine what the path looks like—is it curvy? Or straight? Hilly? Flat? Is it wide or narrow, surrounded by trees or by fields? You look down—is the path rocky? Sandy? Is it dirt? Maybe it's paved. What does it feel like under your feet? And up ahead, what's in your path? Does it look clear or are there hurdles in your way?

Something is in your hands. You've been carrying it a long time—it's something you brought with you, in your spirit, up to camp. Look at it. What does it look like? What does it feel like in your hands? Is it hot? Cold? Warm? Is it smooth? Prickly? Sharp? Rough? Is it heavy or light?

Now look up ahead. A figure is moving toward you. You can't quite make out who it is, but he seems to know you and his pace quickens as he recognizes you. Now you can see—it's Jesus! He's coming closer. What's the expression on his face as he walks toward you? How do you feel? He says a word of greeting to you—what does he say? How do you feel? Do you say anything back?

Now Jesus is standing in front of you. What does he say? Now he's holding his hands out—he wants you to put what's in your hands into his hands. How does it feel as the object leaves your hands? Do you say anything to Jesus?

Now you and Jesus start to walk together—he's holding the object of yours. As the two of you walk along, what do you talk about? Imagine the conversation….

Twenty years later I can still remember the experience of making that discursive meditation before the campers arrived. The feeling of having Jesus take a burden I'd been carrying around was an enormous comfort to me at age 15, and it still is today.

Individuals may also practice discursive meditation by slowly reading a biblical scene repeatedly and then following Ignatius's recommendations for interacting with the scene with all five senses. Again, it's beneficial to journal about the experience afterwards in order to further understand it or at least have a record of the meditation.

Some Christian therapists use meditation in their clinical work, and many loan or sell tapes and CDs to their clients to guide them in a daily meditation. Similar tapes and CDs are available on the Internet, some dealing with specific issues like weight loss and smoking.

A final word

Hans Urs von Balthasar has some words of warning for those of us whose prayers are mainly made up of requests for God:

When in meditation a Christian finds the mystery of God's fullness in his inner divine self-giving, manifested in Jesus Christ, in his Eucharist, and his Church, the Christian too will not find it difficult to find this fullness again in the world so apparently empty of God. If the person does not pray meditatively but only commends personal intentions to God, this refinding will prove to be much more difficult. Perhaps he has succeeded in acquiring a certain Christian disposition in which he makes petitions for himself, his dear ones, and whatever else is important to him without, however, letting himself be sufficiently concerned about God's infinite designs. When Christ requires his disciples to ask in his name (John 14:13), this implies that they must also pray with his universal sentiments, which only a meditating faith can impart.

Sacredspace and Ignation Spiritual Exercises

I'm feeling a little run down today, to be honest. The less-than-24-hour jaunt to Dublin was well worth it, but it left me tired and run down. It's been a couple days now with no exercise and bad food. I just ate a salad in Gatwick Airport as I awaited my flight to Paris, and I'm drinking a bottle of water (always a risk when one doesn't know the bathroom availability).

I was made extremely welcome by the folks at the Jesuit Communication Centre: Alan, Roisin, Mary, Peter, and Mark. I spent a couple hours there, first talking to them all about the state of the Catholic Church—currently a hot topic with all the accusations of pedophilia. Then Alan and I went to his office where he told me about the birth of sacredspace. It's quite interesting.

I went to my hotel, which Alan helped me find, and took a little nap. Then I went back to his office where he interviewed me for a radio program they produce. We went to dinner at the Mao Cafe, and had an excellent conversation about politics, the Ignatian way, Buddhism, and more. At the end of his training as a Jesuit, Alan had spent time in India going through an Examen retreat. Before he returned home, he was encouraged by a friend to go on a 10-day Buddhist retreat. On the first day, all of the participants spent 10 hours sitting still and attending to their breathing, that is, to their nostrils. Ten hours! Successive days were spent attending to other parts of the body, all done in total silence.

With a couple days left, Alan started to feel very anxious. He was truly experiencing things he'd never felt before, and he started to wonder if he should become a Buddhist. Still committed to following Christ, he felt that he had to leave the retreat, which he did even though the master of the retreat did not approve. After that, Alan was quite shaken, a feeling that stayed with him for several years.

After dinner, we went to a pub near Trinity College and had a couple pints of Guinness with some of the young adults who are involved in Sli-Eli, a young adult group formed around the Jesuit Christian Life Community in Dublin. I also met Rory, a Jesuit in his

30s who is director of Sli-Eli. Last week he took 65 young adults on a retreat from Maundy Thursday through Easter. They were broken up into small groups and each small group was given a part of the liturgy over those days—then the small groups led the rest of the group through that portion. They reported that the small groups were very creative, so I plan to follow up with Rory to get more of the details.

This morning has basically been spent traveling...

chapter eight
The Ignatian Examen

*Although we cannot always preserve our recollection,
yet we must do so from time to time, and at least once
a day, either in the morning or in the evening. In the
morning form your intention, and at night examine your
conduct, what you have done, said, and thought during
the day, for in each of these you may have often
offended both God and your neighbor.*

Thomas à Kempis

Father Alan McGuckian is a Jesuit priest and
the former head of the Jesuit Communication
Centre in Dublin, Ireland. In the late 1990s, he
was overseeing a TV production studio and a
radio program when his superiors asked him
to design a website for the Jesuits of Ireland
and England. He set about to do what most of
us would—he planned to develop a site that
would have information for men who were
interested in joining the order, phone numbers,
addresses, and bulletin boards for priests to
share thoughts and ideas.

Being a novice to the Internet, Alan decided to spend some time surfing, getting acquainted with how the Internet works, finding which sites work better than others, and discovering what was most visually attractive. As Alan flipped through webpages, the rhythm reminded him of something: the "gated prayer" he had tried as a novitiate in India. It reminded him of the rhythms of the Ignatian Prayer Examination, upon which Jesuit spiritual life is based.

Alan asked his fellow Jesuit, Peter Scally, if he might be able to design a website that takes people through a daily Ignatian Examen. The result is *sacredspace.ie*, actually a hybrid of Ignatian prayer leading to a *lectio divina* on the lectionary-assigned Scripture passage for the day. *Sacredspace* is translated daily into 17 languages, and it's the top response when you Google "prayer."

As I sat in his office in Dublin, Fr. Alan told me, "Before you go to prayer, consider how God looks at you." In other words, slow down, be quiet, concentrate on your breath in order to calm yourself. On the *sacredspace* site, breathing is one of the first things mentioned, after the encouragement that this form of prayer can be done anywhere — at home, in a cathedral, or in a cubicle.

At the end of a *sacredspace* journey, you're taken to a Web page that shows how many people have visited *sacredspace* (at the time this book went to press, there had been over 10.5 million visitors since the Spring of 1999). I commented to Alan on how overwhelming that number is, and he said, "There is power in the sense of community. *Sacredspace* helps people move from a lonely space into community — prayer always leads people to community."

I asked Alan, a man who has led millions of people in prayer through the Internet, if he had one word of advice for those of us who want to guide others in prayer. He said, "You can't guide other people to pray unless you pray yourself." Amen.

History

Ignatius was born in 1491 in a castle overlooking the city of Loyola, Spain. Raised in nobility, he spent his youth traveling, as many nobles do, learning the arts of literature and warfare, and sinning with abandon. He was devoted to the service of the Spanish king, serving both at court and in the army. In 1517, he joined the Spanish army, and while he was on duty in 1521, his life began to change. He and his troops were defending the city of Pamplona, when a French cannonball passed between his legs, heavily damaging his lower left leg. The French were kind enough to return him to Loyola where he underwent a long convalescence that included re-breaking and setting the leg, sawing off extra bone, and hanging weights from the leg to help it return to its original length.

During his recuperation, he asked for his favorite reading material: tales of chivalrous knights slaying foes and dragons and courting fair maidens. None of these was available, however, so he was instead given a history of the lives of the saints. As he read of the saints fasting and praying, preaching and healing, and of the many who gave their lives for the love of Christ, he noticed a difference in how it affected him: When he read the life of a knight, he ended up feeling dejected and sad, but when he read the life of a saint, he finished with feelings of joy of peace.

Toward the end of his recovery, he saw a vision of the baby Jesus in Mary's arms, and he repented of all his past sins. Feeling that his forgiveness was complete, he began to speak only of spiritual things, and he vowed to serve Christ for the rest of his life.

He left Loyola for Montserrat where he spent three days in the sanctuary of the Benedictine monastery examining his life. Finally, he confessed his sins again, hung his sword on the altar, and put on the clothes of a beggar. In the days that followed, he lived in a nearby cave, praying and wondering if he had truly confessed *all* of his sins, even being tempted to commit suicide. Finally, with God's help he overcame these doubts and emerged from his solitude at peace and full of zeal for God's kingdom.

Ignatius then made a pilgrimage to the Holy Land, all the while taking notes on his spiritual experiences. He spent the next 11 years studying at various universities in Spain and France, often being persecuted for his radically spiritual life (two imprisonments, several beatings, and numerous expulsions from cities). By the end of his studies in Paris, nine men had joined him, and together they made vows of poverty and chastity in 1534. Three years later, this little brotherhood applied to Pope Paul III for official recognition by the Catholic Church, and the Society of Jesus, or Jesuits, was born. By the time of Ignatius's death in 1556, there were about one thousand Jesuits—today there are over 22,000.

Ignatius' *Book of Exercises* was written throughout most of his adult life—he was constantly reworking and revising it. It was published in 1541 and exists today in three early, though not original, editions, one in Spanish and two in Latin. It was written at a time when the Roman Catholic Church was battling the early results of the Protestant Reformation, which added to its relevance and popularity. It has been translated into hundreds of languages, and it constitutes the basis of the Jesuit life. Every Jesuit priest makes a 30-day retreat based on the *Exercises* at least twice during his training for the priesthood, and it serves as the basis of his annual retreat, too.

Theology

The Spiritual Exercises as they come to us today were the result of Ignatius' life work. He led many individuals through the Exercises on retreats throughout his lifetime, and he never stopped examining his own life: "The Exercises come from Ignatius's spiritual journey, characterized by following Jesus, practicing discernment, and acquiring a sense of service."

In Ignatius' own words, he developed "some spiritual exercises by which man is led to the possibility of conquering himself and deciding on a way of conducting his life that is free from harmful attachments." This happens by first examining one's own life in an incredibly thoroughgoing manner, and then meditating on the life, death, and resurrection of Christ. In so doing, individuals are led through confession and repentance to a place where they see Christ in the everyday things of life.

This happens most effectively, Ignatius writes, over the course of four weeks. The four weeks have been described thus:

1. *Deformata reformare* (to reform what has been deformed by sin)
2. *Reformata conformare* (to make what is thus reformed conform to the Divine model, Jesus)
3. *Conformata confirmare* (to strengthen what has been conformed)
4. *Confirmata transformare* (to transform by love the already strengthened resolutions)

The author of Hebrews encourages a similar course of emulating the life of Christ as we shed the sins that bind us:

> *Therefore, since we are surrounded by such a great cloud of witnesses, let us throw off everything that hinders and the sin that so easily entangles, and let us run with perseverance the race marked out for us. Let us fix our eyes on Jesus, the author and perfecter of our faith, who for the joy set before him endured the cross, scorning its shame, and sat down at the right hand of the throne of God.*

Of course, self-examination has been a part of the Jewish-Christian story since close to the beginning. The Hebrews slaugh-

tered a goat, or sent it out into the wilderness, after metaphori-
cally laying their sins on it. Jesus was constantly challenging the
Pharisees to examine not just their actions, but also their hearts.
And Paul was notoriously tough on himself. In the Exercises,
Ignatius developed a method of self-examination that has shaped
hundreds of thousands of lives over the past half millennium.

practice

The *Spiritual Exercises* are written from one retreat director to
other retreat directors. Ignatius didn't write his Exercises for
the individual, and it would be very difficult, if not impossible,
to make the Exercises without a director. The Exercises is full
of notations written to retreat directors on how to treat different
individuals and issues that come up during a retreat. The retreat
director becomes guide, confessor, and accountability partner,
and so it requires a mature and spiritually sound person to fulfill
that role.

The general model of examination is made on the following five
steps:

1. To give thanks to God, our Lord, for all the benefits received
2. To ask for his grace to know and expel our sins
3. To question our soul about the sins committed during the
   day, examining ourselves hour after hour from the time of
   our waking, in thoughts, words, and actions, in the order
   given in the particular examination
4. To ask forgiveness for the faults committed
5. To propose with God's help to correct ourselves; then,
   afterward, to recite the Our Father.

Although Ignatius repeatedly encourages modification of the retreat depending on the advancement of the individual retreatant,
the Exercises are based on a four-week model. Basically, on each
day of the week, the retreatant spends five hour-long sessions
in examination: midnight, dawn, morning, late afternoon, and
evening. During each session, an intricate schedule of prayer,
meditation, and colloquy (conversation with God) is followed. As
you read about these weeks, they may sound extreme and nearly
impossible to practice. Indeed, they are very difficult, especially
in their purest form, but you will see further below that there are
several ways to practice the Exercises in a modified fashion.

During the first week, the retreatant meditates on sins committed, both in action and thought, and imagines confessing these sins

to Jesus as he hangs on the cross. During the fifth exercise of the day, hell is imagined by all five senses as the consequence of the sins committed. Ignatius recommends that during the first week, "I avoid all thoughts that bring me joy...I deprive myself of the brightness of light...I absolutely refrain from laughing...I do not fix my eyes on anyone...[and] I add some kind of reparation or penance...wearing hair shirts, ropes, or chains." He also says the retreatant should have only moderate amounts of sleep and food.

The second week is a contemplation of the life of Jesus Christ, comparing him to an earthly king who is calling his subjects to war. From the first day, meditating on the incarnation and nativity of Jesus, through the final meditation focused on the week leading up to Palm Sunday, the retreatant imagines Lucifer arrayed with all of his forces in one plain, ready to do battle, and Jesus and his forces lined up against him. By the end of this week, Ignatius says the retreatant will be ready to make Election—that is, to choose which army she wants to be a part of, to choose what kind of a person she wants to be.

The Passion of Christ is the focus of the third week. One imagines being at the Last Supper and in the Garden of Gethsemene, at the foot of the cross, and laying Jesus' body in the tomb. Ignatius tells us to imagine the conversation at the Last Supper, how and what the disciples ate, and how it felt to have your feet washed by the Lord. He also suggests abstaining from all food and drink except bread and water during the third week.

Central to the fourth week is the contemplation on Christ's post-resurrection appearances and the joy and victory they signify. It culminates in the contemplation for achieving Divine Love. In this series of contemplations, Ignatius points the retreatant towards a mystical appreciation of the Divine Love that permeates and holds all reality. As a response to all of God's activity, in creation and redemption, the following prayer of complete self-surrender is proposed:

> *Take, Lord, all my freedom. Accept all my memory, intellect, and will. All that I have or possess, you have given to me; all I give back to you, and give up then to be governed by your will. Grant me only the grace to love you, and I am sufficiently rich so that I do not ask for anything else.*

The *Spiritual Exercises* concludes with dozens of notes on praying and on the Christian life.

Some think it should be the goal of every Christian to make the Exercises at some point in life. For those of us with jobs or families, it can be difficult to think of extracting ourselves for 30 days, but it is, of course, a matter of enormous commitment. Around the world, retreat centers and monasteries are always leading Ignatian retreats, some 30 days, but many shorter, too.

And there are alternative ways to examine oneself in an Ignatian fashion. At Georgetown Prep School in North Bethesda, Maryland, the senior boys are given the chance to spend a semester working through the Exercises according to the Nineteenth Annotation, in which Ignatius gives another method for working through the Exercises. Each young man is assigned a guide who is familiar with the Exercises. The adult guides the student through the Exercises with four 20-minute prayer sessions each week. Some make it through the first section of Ignatius' four "weeks," and others make it through more.

More immediately, we might access the three methods of prayer that Ignatius outlines after week four. The first is a slow prayer in which an individual examines his life according to the Ten Commandments, the seven deadly sins, the three faculties of the soul (will, understanding, and memory), and the five senses. To begin, one contemplates the first commandment, confessing every time he has broken it. Upon running out of sins to confess, he says the Lord's Prayer and moves on to the second commandment.

The second method is to take a familiar prayer like the Lord's Prayer and spend one hour meditating on a word or two ("Our Father"). At the end of the hour, one quickly says the rest of the prayer. The next day, the meditation is on the next word or two ("who art"), and so on. The third method of praying combines the first two using the breath as the guide for meditation.

Another application is to rethink the way we normally do things. Often, when church-based small groups meet, before getting to the lesson the group members go around the circle and tell about their "highs and lows" of the last week; a similar event takes place around some family dinner tables. Ignatius' version of this practice is to see life in terms of "consolations" and "desolations," (also translated "enlivening" and "stifling" of God's Spirit). A consolation is "when the soul takes fire in the love of its Creator by some inner motion…any increase of faith, hope, and charity can also be called consolation; equally all joyfulness, which usually incites the soul to meditation on heavenly things, to zeal for salvation, to be at rest and peace with God."

"On the contrary," Ignatius writes, "any obscuring of the soul, any disturbance, any instigation to inferior or earthly things, must be called spiritual desolation." Moments in which we feel far from God, doubt the Spirit's work in our lives, doubt our salvation, or doubt even the existence of God are desolations.

So, instead of measuring the week according to the fairly superficial "highs and lows" of what made us feel good and what didn't, we can examine the past week according to when the Spirit was moving or flowing in their lives versus when the Spirit was blocked or seemed far away. While many of the instances cited by students may be the same as what they would say for "highs and lows," "consolations and desolations" reorients the focus to be on God instead of on self. And this practice can sacralize the otherwise mundane moments in life.

A final word

A prayer from the *Spiritual Exercises:*

> Here I am, O supreme King and Lord of all things, I, so unworthy, but still confiding on your grace and help, I offer myself entirely to you and submit all that is mine to your will. In the presence of your infinite Goodness, and under the sight of your glorious Virgin Mother and of the whole heavenly court, I declare that this is my intention, my desire, and my firm decision: Provided it will be for your greatest praise and for my best obedience to you, to follow you as nearly as possible and to imitate you in bearing injustices and adversities, with true poverty, of spirit and things as well, if it pleases your holiest Majesty to elect and accept me for such a stage of life.

Boiler Room/Jesus Prayer

So it turns out that the whole reason to practice spiritual disciplines is to overcome my overwhelming proclivity to sin. (Of course, that's overstated—they also help me to move closer to God and to be more prepared to serve God's creation.) The more I fill my mind and body with the things of God, the less I'll be tempted to think about/act on the things that pull me away from God. What's amazing is how quickly my mind and my body move toward sin when I veer from the disciplines.

Everything in my American bloodstream, everything in my DirecTV, two-car-three-bedroom-one-and-three-quarter-bath DNA is repelled by the disciplines. Take for instance the daily office. No one's going to tell me that I have to stop three times a day to think on God, to pray a rite, to be reminded of my sin! Or the Jesus Prayer—how boring! But, as I've gotten into both of these disciplines on my sabbatical, I find such comfort in the routine, the simplicity. No more searching about how to guide my prayer. No more wondering about what form to pray in. No more worrying that I hadn't spent enough time adoring or confessing or thanking or supplicating.

Last night I was given the midnight - 2 a.m. shift to pray at the Boiler Room. I think I did pretty well. Of course, I floated in and out of concentration, but I worked really hard to be disciplined. If I caught myself fading, I moved right back into the prayer. For the first 30 minutes, I prayed the Jesus Prayer and I think I found a breathing rhythm that will work for me: Breathing in: Lord Jesus Christ, Son of the Living God; breathing out: Have mercy on me, a sinner. Then I went online and prayed through the Sacred Space prayer for the day. After that I took a break, ate a snack, drank some water, and walked around for a few minutes.

When I went back to the prayer room, I started through the Psalms. When I found my mind wandering, I'd switch translations—from the Message to the NRSV (on my Palm) to the BCP (also on the Palm).

Finally, the alarm on my Palm went off at 1:45 and I prayed Compline. Then I woke up Malcolm for his shift and I went to bed. The two hours passed quite quickly.

chapter nine
ICONS

*We must revere Christ above all things, and live
purely in his sight as angels.*

Thomas à Kempis

Frederica Mathewes-Green is a truly awesome
writer; she also happens to be Orthodox and
married to an Antiochian Orthodox priest, so
she's done a lot of thinking and writing about
the traditions of Eastern Christian spirituality,
most recently, *The Open Door: Entering the
Sanctuary of Icons and Prayer,* a wonderful
journey into an Orthodox sanctuary. Frederica
and I have corresponded for the last several
years, so I asked her to reflect on the meaning
of icons to begin this chapter:

> The first thing we sense about an icon is its
> great seriousness. Compare an icon in your
> mind with a great Western religious painting,
> one that moves you to deeper faith or even to
> tears. You'll notice that there is a difference
> in the *way* it moves you, however. A Western

painting—which is undeniably going to be more accomplished in terms of realism, perspective, lighting, anatomy, and so forth— moves us in our imaginations and our emotions. We engage with it like we do a movie or a story.

An icon hits us in a different way, though. In comparison, it is very still. It is silent. We find ourselves coming to silence as we stand before it. An icon somehow takes command of the space around it. It re-sets the baseline of our awareness.

Many years ago my husband bought our first icon, a copy of the famous twelfth century Russian icon known as the Virgin of Vladimir. We hung it on a wall in the den and grouped other, smaller, pictures and paintings around it. But it never looked quite right. We kept rearranging the pictures, and then started taking some of them down. It still didn't work somehow. In the end, we wound up taking down every other painting, so that the Virgin reigned alone in that length of space. She blew all the other pictures off the wall. Such is the quality of her presence in this image, a quality we can't describe apart from words like "majesty," "mystery," and "gravity."

It is the gravity of an icon that is the other thing I want you to notice. The people in these images are very sober. Their silence is unsettling. We don't know how to respond and feel awkward. I think this is something like what St. Peter felt when the Lord told him to let down his nets for a catch. When he hauled up teeming nets, St. Peter said, "Depart from me, for I am a sinful man, O Lord."

The sober presence of the Lord in an icon makes us uncomfortable because it makes us realize how far short we fall from the ineffable beauty and power of God. Sometimes people accuse Christians of trying to make people feel bad or guilty, of being judgmental in their words. When that is the case it is unfortunate. But in this case, we feel the effect of judgment from the only true judge, the only possible judge, and he does it without a word. Yet it is a judgment wrapped in a promise of healing. It is not a rejection, but an invitation. It is an opportunity to receive the healing that only God can give, because he knows us better than we know ourselves.

The steady, unsettling gaze of the Lord in an icon is like the gaze of a surgeon as he looks at a patient's wounded, broken body. The surgeon understands the woundedness better than the patient does, and he knows exactly what it will take to heal it. Our Lord sees brokenness and failures in us that we can't, that we simply won't, that we could not bear to see. And he invites us to open ourselves to his healing, a healing that will progress very gently, very gradually, as we are able to bear it.

This isn't to say that the healing will always be comfortable. He may ask us to give things up that we think we can't bear to live without. He may ask us to take things on that we think we can't begin to carry. Only he knows what it will take to heal us. No wonder an icon looks so serious. Our condition is serious. Through the merciful condescension of our Lord, we don't have to enter into healing with a surgeon we have never seen. He has revealed his face to us, and as we gradually learn to trust him, we can reveal our own broken selves in return.

History

According to legend, the first icon (*icon* is Greek for 'image') was made by Jesus himself. In an extrabiblical story kept alive by the church, King Abgar of Edessa was dying of leprosy in North Africa and sent an emissary, Ananias, to ask Jesus to come to Edessa and heal him. Ananias was instructed to paint a picture of Jesus if a visit to Edessa was not possible. Jesus declined traveling to Edessa, for he was only days away from his Passion, but when he saw Ananias trying to paint his picture through the heavy crowds, Jesus took pity on him. After washing his face, Jesus dried his face with a square of linen, leaving a near-perfect imprint of his image on the cloth.

Ananias took the linen back to Edessa and King Abgar was healed immediately upon seeing it. After Pentecost, Thaddeus (a.k.a. St. Jude) took a missionary journey to Edessa, and Edessa became the first officially Christian nation in the late second century. The *acheiropoietos* (ak-air-o-póy-a-tos), the "icon made without human hands", stayed in Edessa until 951, when it was sent to Constantinople to heal the ailing Emperor Romanus. In 1204, Constantinople was sacked by the Crusaders and the famous icon was taken to Italy. Its whereabouts today are unknown.

In similar stories, St. Luke, a physician and, according to legend, a painter, painted five portraits of Mary while she was still alive. One of these, an icon of Mary with the baby Jesus, was given to her as a gift. And, as we observe in the Stations of the Cross, another tradition has Veronica (*vera icona*, "true image") handing Jesus a cloth to wipe his face as he carried his Cross to Golgotha—this icon is kept in one of the massive piers that supports the cupola of St. Peter's basilica in Rome. The Shroud of Turin (supposedly the linen in which Jesus was wrapped in the tomb), the authenticity of which is often debated, is another such legendary object.

All of these stories tie the origin of iconography to Jesus himself. And, indeed, there is much to suggest that, even if these stories are all fictional, portraits of Jesus were painted while those who knew him were still alive. Second-century Christians painted many images, though none of Jesus, in the catacombs of Rome and throughout the Empire. Mosaic and carved wooden representations of Jesus survive in Rome from the fourth century, and St. Catherine's monastery at the base of Mt. Sinai has traditional icons of Jesus and Peter dating from the sixth century. Jim Forest notes that iconographers often used brighter paint to spruce up images that had gotten dark and dirty over the years; he piques our imaginations with this suggestion: "Perhaps at the foundation level of one or another ancient icon are brush strokes that were made by the hand of St. Luke."

Icons have always held an important place in the imagination and faith of Eastern Christians. While some of the early church fathers condemned the use of icons, the people, never altogether impressed with theological battles, made icons a central aspect of their practice of Christianity. The painting and reproduction of icons became more formalized in the second half of the first millennium, and their use was known across the Eastern world.

Icons also came under attack during this time. Some theologians questioned whether praying to icons actually constituted idolatry, forbidden by the Second Commandment. Others merely found it distasteful that someone would try to capture the infinite God in a painting. In the first half of the eighth century, Emperor Leo III believed that the use of icons had gotten out of control, and he thought their use was an obstacle to the evangelism of Jews and Muslims. In 726 he issued an edict ordering the destruction of all icons. Although his actions were condemned by the pope and persuasively put down in a theological treatise by John of Damascus, the "Iconoclastic Controversy" continued until 784. During that time, thousands of icons were destroyed, iconographers had their hands chopped off, and many monks fled to the West with icons hidden under their robes.

Empress Irene, who loved icons, convened the Seventh General Council of the church in Nicaea in 787. The council undid Leo's edict, set parameters on the veneration and painting of icons, and decreed the restoration of icons throughout the empire. The "Second Iconoclastic Controversy" broke out under Leo V and lasted another 28 years. Only in 843 were icons finally restored, and on the first Sunday of Lent that year, a great feast was held to celebrate the end of the controversy. To this day, the Eastern church celebrates the first Sunday of Lent as the "Feast of the Triumph of Orthodoxy."

In the East, the Iconoclastic Controversies among the educated clergy actually caused an increase in the use of icons among the masses. But in the West, there was great confusion about the theology behind the use of icons, mostly attributed to a mistranslation of the Acts of the Nicene Council. Sadly, this confusion combined with the other theological and political frictions that eventually led to the Great Schism between East and West in 1054. To this day, icons are very significant in the theology of the Eastern Church, yet they are only now gaining popularity in the West.

Theology

Most of the theological controversies and heresies of the early church (and many today) centered on the nature of Christ: Was he truly human? Was he truly divine? Was he more divine than he was human, or more human than he was divine? All sorts of cults and sects sprang up in the first five centuries of Christianity, each claiming to have the truth about Christ's true nature. And all of the top theologians rose to the challenge of rearticulating what Paul had made clear in his epistles: through some miraculous paradox, Jesus of Nazareth was fully human and fully divine. When defending the painting and use of icons, St. John of Damascus and others argued on the basis of this very idea. If the second person of the Trinity, the Logos, became Jesus of Nazareth, and if Jesus of Nazareth was a real human being, then he could, and indeed should be represented in paintings. In his treatise defending iconography, John of Damascus wrote:

> If we made an image of the invisible God, we would certainly be in error...but we do not do anything of the kind; we do not err, in fact, if we make the image of God incarnate who appeared on the earth in the flesh, who in his ineffable goodness, lived with men and assumed the nature, the volume, the form, and the color of the flesh.

Simon Jenkins, a modern writer, agrees:

> The point about icons is that they affirm the teaching, to quote the language of the Creed, that Jesus Christ is "the only-begotten Son of God" who "was made man." Simply to paint an image of Christ is to confess that Jesus, the Son of God, truly appeared on earth as a human being — "sprung from Mary as

well as from God," in the words of St. Ignatius. It is to confess that "the Word
made flesh" could be seen with the eyes. And conversely, to oppose the making of
icons is to deny that confession.... [I]cons stand on the front line of
the faith: they stand or fall on the truth of Christianity itself.

But even if the painting of a portrait of Jesus can be justified
theologically, what of the real danger that, when that portrait is an
icon, it actually becomes an idol? To answer this question, we have
to investigate an intricacy of Orthodox theology: the difference
between *adoration* and *veneration*. Adoration is that form of human
submission and worship that is due only to Almighty God. Adoration is what a creature gives the Creator. Adoration is worship.

Veneration, on the other hand, is how one uses an icon in
prayer—not unlike the Bible, which we venerate and respect,
but don't worship. The Bible brings us closer to God, guides us
in prayer, and is considered a gift from God, even though it was
written and translated by human hands. Similarly, an icon, painted by human hands, leads us into God's presence. In fact, the
Nicene Council of 787 stated that it's not the icon that is venerat-
ed, but the ideal and perfect prototype on which the icon is based.
Similarly, we might say we don't venerate the New International
Version or the Message translations but the ways in which they
draw us to Jesus Christ, the living Word, and to God.

Another example of this difference is the Catholic belief that
Christians can pray *through* saints, especially the Blessed Virgin
Mary, and their prayers will be delivered to the throne of God. I'll
admit that, to a Protestant like me, the difference between praying
through an icon or a saint is a nuance I have a hard time grasping.
However, I can understand the theological difference, and I respect the traditions under which they have developed. The bottom
line is that we use icons to pray, but we pray *through* them, not *to*
them. In this case, the preposition makes all the difference.

Father Nicholas Speier of Goleta, California, explained it to me
like this: I ask friends to pray for me; in fact, I even ask friends on
the phone, whom I cannot see, to pray for me. Since we believe
that those who have died in faith are currently living in eternity
with God, praying through an icon of a saint is simply asking one
of these friends to pray for me.

practice

In order to incorporate praying with icons into your personal
devotional life, the first item of business is to get an icon. They

are sold at many Orthodox churches and monasteries and they can also be ordered on the Internet. True icons are made in accordance with a very specific set of rules. Most often they are painted on a wooden panel, using egg yolk-based tempura paint. A piece of linen is stretched over the wood, which acts as a canvas. Linseed oil is applied after the paint has dried to protect the image.

A limited number of poses are available to the iconographer, all stemming from the ancient icons — for instance, the portrait of Jesus' face alone is a replica of "The Icon Made without Human Hands"; and the "Icon of Loving-Kindness" shows the baby Jesus with his face pressed against his mother's and was supposedly first painted by St. Luke. Human models are never used to paint icons; only other icons are acceptable as models.

Shadows are never seen in an icon, and no source of light illuminates the subject's face. The icon itself is a source of light: "The saintliness or the holiness of the person shines out from the entire body. The light of God saturates all things, therefore, the images on icons do not cast shadows." The parts of the anatomy associated with the five senses are exaggerated in size, since they are the windows to the soul, and the person in the icon looks straight ahead at the pray-er. Backgrounds are used only to identify the saint, so most icons of Jesus or Mary have no scenery.

Both the figures and the minimal scenery in an icon seem strange, even awkward, to modern eyes. However an icon is not meant to be a depiction of a normal human being but of Jesus or Mary or a saint in their resurrected state — what St. Paul calls a "spiritual body" and theologians call a "resurrection body." Reality is not the artist's goal. Neither is the icon meant to draw the viewer into a scene. Instead, the focal point of the icon is actually in front of the painting, where the viewer is standing, so an icon can be thought of as embracing the pray-er. Henri Nouwen once said:

Icons are not easy to "see." They do not immediately speak to our senses. They do not excite, fascinate, stir our emotions, or stimulate our imagination. At first, they even seem somewhat rigid, lifeless, schematic, and dull. They do not reveal themselves to us at first sight. It is only gradually, after patient, prayerful presence that they start speaking to us. And as they speak, they speak more to our inner than to our outer senses. They speak to the heart that searches for God.

Iconographers fast and pray while they are painting, making the creation of an icon a spiritual experience itself. Finally, if the image meets all the criteria, it's blessed by a priest and is ready for display in a church or home.

In an Orthodox church, icons are displayed on an *iconostasis*, a large screen that runs the width of the sanctuary and separates the sanctuary (where worshipers sit) from the nave (where the altar resides). As with most other aspects of Orthodox ecclesiology, the *iconostasis gives a church an otherworldly and mysterious feel.*

Most devout Orthodox families and individuals also have an "icon corner" in their homes, always on an Eastern wall so they will be facing Jerusalem if Jesus returns while they are at prayer. Actually, this practice is becoming more popular with all types of Christians—devoting some area of the home as "sacred space" with a candle, an icon or two, and a prayer book. One can then stop once, or several times a day, and pray using the icon, whether it's a prayer from a book kept in the corner or an extemporaneous outpouring. The icon corner can also be an excellent place for a family to gather daily or weekly for devotions.

One would be hard-pressed to argue against the fact that we live in an image-saturated world. While Christianity is a faith based on the written word of Scripture, we must take seriously our image-based lives. One way to do this is to incorporate icons into our lives, for, "We do not have to be passive victims of a world that wants to entertain and distract us. We can make some decisions and choices. A spiritual life in the midst of our energy-draining society requires us to take conscious steps to safeguard that inner space where we can keep our eyes fixed on the beauty of the Lord."

As with any spiritual practice, if the use of icons is outside of your tradition, it's advisable to enter cautiously and respectfully into another's tradition—cautiously because others in your church or family may not understand or agree, and respectfully so as not to offend those Christians for whom icon-based prayer is central to faith.

A final word

In his defense of icons, St. John of Damascus said:

> *Previously there was absolutely no way in which God, who has neither a body nor a face, could be represented by any image. But now that he has made himself visible in the flesh and has lived with people, I can make an image of what I have seen of God...and contemplate the glory of the Lord, his face having been unveiled.*

And a bonus from Henri Nouwen:

Icons...have imprinted themselves so deeply on my inner life that they appear every time I need comfort and consolation. There are many times when I cannot pray, when I am too tired to read the gospels, too restless to have spiritual thoughts, too depressed to find words for God, or too exhausted to do anything. But I can still look at these images so intimately connected with the experience of love.

Pilgrimage/Daily Office

The journey home, too, is a pilgrimage of sorts. Bus, train, bus, plane, plane—that's the order this time. I've determined to tell my fellow travelers the type of journey I'm on this time, and let them think what they will. Reactions vary, but most people are interested.

On the ninth day of sabbatical, I'm really falling in love with praying the Daily Office, particularly the prayers said before bed at Compline. To pray for all those "who watch, work, and weep this night...for the sick...for the dying...for the grieving." Those prayers really serve to put life in perspective, especially at the end of what I would consider a long and grueling day, but I am reminded every night before I fall asleep that hospitals are full; that parents, spouses, children, and friends grieve; and that others have needs that are far more difficult than mine.

chapter ten
spiritual direction

Do not flatter the wealthy, and avoid the society of the great. Associate rather with the humble and simple, the devout, and the virtuous, and converse with them on such things as edify.

Thomas à Kempis

Beth Slevcove is a spiritual director in California, and she also helps pastors around the country find spiritual directors for themselves. She wrote this about her experience of getting started with direction:

When I first met Sister Bunny, I had no idea what to expect. I had never met with a spiritual director before, never talked with a Catholic nun, and never met anyone named Bunny. I was nervous.

As we talked I began to share some of the goings-on in my life (prayer life, relationships, school). She asked a couple questions about where I was noticing God in it all, and that was it. No huge "Ahas", no life-changing moments, just a conversation, a listening ear, and some questions. I tried another spiritual director.

Same thing happened.

My "What should I do?" was responded to with a "Where do you sense God in that?" I met with spiritual director number three. This time a Presbyterian. Certainly she'll give me some answers.

Nope, same thing..."How is God drawing you out in that situation?"

My husband is the one who started to notice subtle changes in me. Something was happening in the periods between my spiritual direction sessions. God was somehow, subtly, slowly, and in the most ordinary of ways forming my heart and mind through these very questions that I found so irritating. It finally began to dawn on me that these were exactly the questions I want to live my life by. These are the questions that pull me out of my narcissistic world and into the greater world for which God has created me.

Something broken in me keeps telling me if I just work harder, read more Scripture, and become a better pray-er, God will be pleased and perhaps my life will be easier. This misconception and the myriad of other false beliefs that not-so-occasionally reek havoc in my body and brain are called out into the light when I seek spiritual direction. I notice God at work in places I hadn't considered and in ways I hadn't imagined.

Meeting with a spiritual director has reminded me of the deepest realities I know, and yet, the ones I so quickly forget: Namely that God is already at work here in my life and in this world; and that God is the initiator of all healing, redemption, wholeness, conviction, abundance; and I am the one who is invited to respond, and to partner.

What started as curiosity, then pure discipline, has become a tender resting place in my journey through this world. It has become like a wayside chapel on a pilgrimage route where the weary pilgrim seeks sustenance and rest for body and soul.

As a spiritual director, I now get to be present with others in a way that encourages them on their journey of faith. I get to be the one asking the annoying questions, the God-hunting questions. I also continue to be a directee, where once a month I stop and rest in the presence of God with another, where I am encouraged to honestly reflect on my life in all its peace and chaos, and where I am reminded of God's work and loving presence in the midst of it all.

History

We all might long for the spiritual direction that Adam received when he walked with God in the garden "at the time of the

evening breeze." We can only imagine that kind of direct
guidance from the Lord. But we live east of Eden, and that kind
of direction isn't available to us. Fortunately, the Bible is rife
with examples of spiritual companionship, both good and bad.
From the spiritual friendship between David and Jonathan to
the highly suspect advice of Job's "theologian" friends, Scripture
gives some parameters for healthy spiritual direction.

One paradigmatic example takes place in the story of the
prophet Samuel. When the young Samuel is confused by the
voice he hears in the night, Eli, Samuel's spiritual father, "realized that the Lord was calling the boy." The Lord was moving in
Samuel's life, speaking to him, in fact, but it took another who
was older and more experienced in the movements of God to
open Samuel's eyes and ears to God.

Of course, the paramount example of spiritual direction is
Jesus himself. A model of friendship, Jesus spent time with his
disciples both individually and in groups. He asked questions,
told stories, and guided his friends, sometimes gently and sometimes forcefully, toward the truth. In all things, he showed charity, love, and a deep desire for these men and women to grow
spiritually. His guidance was not self-serving. He listened, both to
things spoken and unspoken (for instance, the Samaritan woman
at the well). He pointed to the movements of the Holy Spirit. He
was called "Good Teacher."

The Desert Fathers and Mothers got their titles, *Abba* and
Amma, from offering this kind of guidance. As the reputation of
the mystics on Mt. Athos and in the Egyptian and Syrian deserts
grew, hundreds, even thousands of lay people and clerics made
pilgrimages to see them. The Desert Fathers and Mothers considered it part of their vocation to lead their visitors into deeper holiness, to teach them the ways of contemplative prayer, and even to
look into their lives with the insight of divine discernment. "You
must prostrate yourselves before brothers who come to visit you,"
Abba Apollo said, "for it is not them but God you venerate."

Their teaching might seem off-putting to us. In another incident,
Abba Isaac went to two different elder Fathers hoping for spiritual
guidance, but they served him instead of giving him advice. Out
of frustration, he asked what he must do to receive some spiritual
direction, and the elder Abba answered him (speaking of Isaac in
the third person), "As far as I am concerned, I do not tell him anything, but if he wishes he can do what he sees me doing." And so
Isaac learned to work in silence just as he saw this Father working

in silence. In any case, it was expected that every Abba or Amma was under the tutelage of another Abba or Amma.

In the twelfth century, Aelred of Rievaulx (1109-1166) wrote *Spiritual Friendship*. In it he commends a prototype for companions in spirit:

> *What happiness, what security, what joy to have someone to whom you dare to speak on terms of equality as to another self; one to whom you can unblushingly make known what progress you have made in the spiritual life; one to whom you can entrust all the secrets of your heart and before whom you can place all your plans.*

In both Eastern Orthodox and Roman Catholic traditions, spiritual direction has been common among laity and mandatory among clergy. Recently, Protestants have become very interested in the practice, flocking to Catholic seminaries to earn certificates in spiritual direction. More Protestant seminaries are offering similar certificates, evangelical publishers are producing books on the subject, and several Protestant centers for spiritual direction have opened.

Clearly, over the years spiritual direction has taken on a more formal shape than when a believer sat at the feet of Jesus or of an Abba or Amma. But at its heart, spiritual direction attempts to recreate that same environment in which Adam walked with God: a time of peace and listening to discover where God is moving in one's life.

Theology

God was Adam's companion. Joshua looked to Moses. Ruth placed herself under Naomi's direction. Elisha learned from Elijah. The disciples followed Jesus. Timothy was Paul's companion. Peter walked the streets of Jerusalem with John. There is no dearth of examples in Scripture of one person giving spiritual companionship to another.

But beyond that, spiritual direction is reliant upon a theology of the Holy Spirit. The belief implicit in spiritual direction is that God's Spirit is alive and active in the world, constantly moving in the believer's life. The second premise is that believers who are experienced in life and faith and who are committed to spiritual disciplines themselves may be able to help others to notice the movements of the Spirit.

Most of the practices outlined in this book combat the noisiness of our world, and spiritual direction is no different. Because our lives are so quickly crowded with work responsibilities, kids' games and band concerts, and family vacations, many of us need to schedule a time once or twice a month to meet with a spiritual director.

It will help to define spiritual direction by noting what it's *not*:

> *Spiritual direction is not psychotherapy nor is it an inexpensive substitute, although the disciplines are compatible and frequently share raw material. Spiritual direction is not pastoral counseling, nor is it to be confused with the mutuality of deep friendships…. [I]n this covenanted relationship the director has agreed to put himself aside so that his total attention can be focused on the person sitting in the other chair. What a gift to bring to another, the gift of disinterested, loving attention!*

Although Jesus was surely "better" and "holier" than his disciples, the director-directee relationship attempts to mimic the Jesus-disciple relationship in a way that therapy, mentoring, and even pastoral counseling do not. Therapy and pastoral counseling most often takes place because of a crisis in life—a counselor or pastor helps someone through the crisis, applying psychological techniques, accumulated wisdom, and possible Scripture to the issue at hand. Persons seeking spiritual direction, on the other hand, are looking for God, wanting to be held accountable in their prayer practices, and attempting to discern the Spirit in their lives. "In my view," says Eugene Peterson, "spiritual direction is a conversation in which…the person [is taken] seriously as a soul, as a creation of God for whom prayer is the most natural language."

The *Catholic Encyclopedia* may say it best, under the assumption that all Christians are to strive for spiritual perfection, as both Jesus and Paul commended us to do, and a spiritual director's job is to guide the directee in that pursuit of perfection:

> *This striving after Christian perfection means the cultivation of certain virtues and watchfulness against faults and spiritual dangers. The knowledge of this constitutes the science of asceticism. The spiritual director must be well versed in this difficult science, as his advice is very necessary for such souls. For, as Cassian writes, "by no vice does the devil draw a monk headlong and bring him to death sooner than by persuading him to neglect the counsel of the Elders and trust to his own judgment and determination."*

Whereas the Orthodox and Catholic traditions emphasize a hierarchical model of spiritual direction that reflects their ecclesiology, an equally significant model is currently emerging in Protestant circles. In this model, the SD isn't necessarily older or more experienced than the directee. Instead, the director is seen primarily as a companion on the spiritual journey—one who is committed to taking time to listen to the spiritual goings-on of the directee. The underlying belief is that God communicates directly with us. Thus, the director is not an expert who speaks for God, but one who helps others notice God's communication with them. "[T]he sheep listen to his voice. He calls his own sheep by name and leads them out."

One of my past SDs used this metaphor: "We're like two people sitting on a train; I'm in the aisle seat, you're in the window seat, and you are describing to me what you see." Another SD likens it to a triangle where the bottom two corners represent the director and the directee and the top corner is the Holy Spirit, Jesus, or God (the *true* directors). "I sit on the same level as the directee as we together pay attention and listen to God," she told me. She compares this understanding of direction to Paul's statements that the church is the *body* of Christ, and the Lord is the *head* of this body.

practice

The growth and professionalization of spiritual direction is a recent phenomenon. Something that had been done more or less informally since the time immemorial has become formalized in structure and training. Nowadays, many Protestant spiritual directors are current or former pastors and others are laypeople, while Catholic SDs continue most often to be monks, nuns, and priests, and the tradition of having a *starets* (Russian for "spiritual father") is still common in the Orthodox church. Most spiritual directors have received formal training, either while in seminary or later, and they combine that with years of pastoral and spiritual experience. While some people like to follow the Orthodox tradition of an older, wiser SD, others value youth and the corresponding lack of predisposition in a younger SD.

You can find an SD in the Yellow Pages, but it's better to call a monastery in your vicinity—both Benedictine and Franciscan monasteries usually have SDs available. (The Resource section in the back of this book has some links for finding an SD.)

Choosing an SD takes some patience. There should be a good vibe between the two of you, and you should have an inherent respect for your director's faith journey. Since spiritual direction isn't a forum for debating theology, it often doesn't matter if the director is from a different Christian tradition than you, but you may want to look for someone with whom you share an affinity. My past SD is a former pastor who spent 16 years on the staff of a large church—but someone else might want an SD from a totally different type of church than his own. Spiritual directors are trained in theology, Christian spirituality, church history, discernment, and listening skills. When looking for an SD, seek out someone who is Christ-centered, discerning, compassionate, and honest about her or his journey of faith.

Spiritual direction should not be romanticized—the sessions are rarely extraordinary. Good spiritual direction is actually quite ordinary. Here's what Eugene Peterson says to the pastor/spiritual director about that ordinariness:

> *I have two basic definitions of spiritual direction. One is you show up and then you shut up. It's important that people have a place they can come to and know that you're going to be there with and for them. The other is that spiritual direction largely involves what you do when you don't think you're doing anything. You're not answering a question, and it doesn't seem like you're doing anything. It takes a lot of restraint and discipline.*

Most SDs have hour-long sessions, and they may charge anywhere from $35 to $65 per meeting—once or twice a month is normal. Sessions often start with just a moment or two of chitchat and then silence. At first I thought, *I'm paying to sit in silence!* But then I came to find the silence an appropriate and peaceful way to begin. Most often the directee breaks the silence and the conversation flows from there. Most SDs don't take notes—another difference between SDs and therapists or pastoral counselors—but a good director will remember past dialogues and bring to light the thread of God's Spirit woven between them. In the end, each person's experience of spiritual direction is unique, a blessed chemistry between director and directee.

I also want to note that I've emphasized the currently popular model of hiring a professional SD. As Eugene Peterson has argued, this is also an oft-neglected role of the pastor, who is paid by the church. Finally, many of us have deep friendships that

more easily fall into the category of Aelred's "spiritual friendship."
Pastors and friends can both serve as spiritual directors, either
formally or informally, but it seems to work best on a formal
basis. Even with a friend, the more formal you can make it, the
better: for example, "We'll meet twice a year for two days each
and take turns directing one another." Without the deliberate
direction in the relationship, even the best Christian friends do
not fall under either the ancient or modern definition of spiritual
direction.

final word

Aelred of Rievaulx wrote this about *Spiritual Friendship*, and it is a
beautiful picture of the heart of spiritual direction:

> *A friend is called a guardian of love or as some would have it, a guardian of the*
> *spirit itself. Since it is fitting that my friend be a guardian of our mutual love or*
> *the guardian of my own spirit so as to preserve all its secrets in faithful silence,*
> *let him, as far as he can, cure and endure such defects as he may observe in it; let*
> *him rejoice with his friend in his joys and weep with him in his sorrows and feel*
> *as his own all that his friend experiences.*

Lectio Divina

Today, in a group lectio, we read and heard the passage
Isaiah 43:1-2:

But now thus says the LORD, he who created you, O Jacob, he
who formed you, O Israel: Do not fear, for I have redeemed you;
I have called you by name, you are mine. When you pass through
the waters, I will be with you; and through the rivers, they shall not
overwhelm you; when you walk through fire you shall not be burned,
and the flame shall not consume you.

What I heard over and over was, "I have redeemed you." I
focused, thought, prayed, and listened. Of that phrase, the word
"redeemed" kept coming up, and I really tried to think about what
redeemed means in its theological sense, and what it means to me
personally.

While that was fruitful, far more powerful was just letting the
phrase, "I have redeemed you" wash over me. That's probably the
best way I can describe it—washing over me like a kind of baptism.
I took a long walk and, in my mind, repeated the phrase over and
over, dozens of time, one word per step: I...have...redeemed...you...
It was a long and deliberate walk. I couldn't go very quickly,
since I was repeating these words. But it was awesome. It was
like, by the end, I truly felt redeemed—like, I actually believe
that he redeemed me!!!

chapter eleven
the Daily office

Desire and pray always that God's will may be perfectly fulfilled in you.

Thomas à Kempis

In the Burgundy region of southern France, there's a village called Taizé. In 1940, Brother Roger arrived there, looking for a place to establish a brotherhood of Catholic and Protestant men who were committed to Christ, to each other, and to peace. The people of Taizé welcomed him warmly, and Brother Roger camped there on the outskirts of the village.

When I arrived there 62 years later, some things had changed dramatically, while others hadn't. Brother Roger was still there, surrounded by a group of 110 brothers who have given up all worldly possessions, including even their inheritances, to Communauté Taizé. They wear simple white cloaks, bound at the waist with a rope. But in the decades since Brother Roger founded the community, they've sent dozens of brothers out to serve in the world, written music that's used everywhere there are Christians, and become *the* major pilgrimage site for young Christians and seekers in Europe.

I made my first pilgrimage to Taizé in April 2002. I met a wide variety of people there: a youth pastor from Virginia with his family, a group of Catholic men in their 40s from Germany, a young woman from Holland. Lise, from Holland, had been at Taizé four times previously and had seen anywhere from about 60 pilgrims there in January to over 7,000 in July.

I was one of about 1,000 pilgrims at Taizé that April. Located in a beautiful area of vineyards and rolling hills, the campus itself isn't particularly luxurious. Pilgrims are encouraged to bring tents, but there are barracks available for a few hundred people. The food is forgettable, stew and a small loaf of crusty bread served in plastic bowls. Dirt paths everywhere complete the rustic feeling of Taizé.

So I was baffled at first about the great attraction of this place, that is, until I went to evening prayers the first night. I got to the *Eglesia* a few minutes early, which was a good thing because hundreds were already gathered there. Seating was all on the floor, although some people got the few hundred kneeling benches scattered around. The church was dimly lit, and scores of candles burned on the altar and around the room.

Right up through the middle of the sanctuary, separated from the rest of the building by planters two feet tall, was a row of chairs and kneelers. One or two at a time, the brothers entered the sanctuary, walking up the middle and taking their places, praying before the service starts. At the appointed time, the bells outside started to ring and Brother Roger entered, walking with the aid of a cane and another brother. On a small screen, a digital readout of the song number flashed; we found our place in the songbook and everyone sang. And then I knew what Taizé is all about. The singing was unlike anything I've ever heard—all these people, most of them under 30, from different countries and different languages, united in song.

The songs are contemplative, sung in many different languages. They're simple tunes that are repeated for five minutes or more each. You never know when a song is going to end and I quit trying to guess pretty quickly. Sometimes after a song ended, there was complete silence—in a way you'd never think 1,000 people could be silent—for maybe 10 minutes. In addition to the singing, the thrice-daily services also include readings—one Scripture passage each day—or the Eucharist—also once per day (holy bread is given to those who do not wish to receive communion).

And so I discovered that the morning, afternoon, and evening prayer services are the lifeblood of Taizé. I cannot describe what happens in that sanctuary other than to say it's something mystical. When I talked to young people who were there for the second, third, or fourth times, they all talked about the worship, which they call "prayer". That's the thing that gets them back, and, indeed, it's the thing that has stuck with me and bounced around in my soul since I made my first pilgrimage.

I returned to Taizé in July, 2003. There I met Maggie, a young German woman who was just ending a six-month stay. I asked her about the allure of Taizé, and she answered, "I stayed so that it would settle down in me. So that it would be not something I do but the very rhythm of my life. It's no longer this place, it's the idea of prayer and rest. I left home looking for freedom, but I take with me freedom on the inside. Taizé is merely the frame—the portrait inside the frame is my life with God."

History

The three daily services of prayer aren't unique to Taizé. In fact, the Daily Office, as it's called, is the common practice that links monasteries and clergy with laity around the world and through the centuries.

The people of God have long considered ordered prayers during the day a practice that pleases God, as the psalmist declares: "Seven times a day I praise you for your righteous laws." Although scholars don't know exactly when these seven times might have been (or if the number is meant literally or figuratively in the tradition of wisdom literature, in which seven is the number of perfection), the Jews under Roman rule were influenced by their rulers. Without clocks being widely accessible, the bell in the forum of a Roman town rang to mark the passing of the day at 6 a.m. (the first hour), 9 a.m. (the third hour), and so on. And so we read of Peter and John "going up to the temple at the time of prayer"—at three in the afternoon (Greek: "the ninth hour"); and, years later, Peter was on a rooftop in Joppa at noon (Greek: "the sixth hour"), when God spoke in his prayer and told him that all animals had been made clean to eat.

Along with the Lord's Supper, fixed-hour prayer is considered the oldest form of Christian spirituality. The apostles used the psalms in their prayers, and the psalms remain the backbone of the Office today. The writer of the *Didache* (ca. A.D. 60) commended the Lord's Prayer to be recited three times per day. Many of the church fathers of the second and third centuries taught the practice of morning and evening prayers, as well as prayers at the third, sixth, and ninth hours. In his *Rule*, Benedict formalized the Offices for his monks, which have continued in this basic form ever since:

- *Matins* (from Latin, "of the morning"): The first Office is held before dawn, keeping vigil for the day to come. Psalms 63 and 95 are often used, and silent prayer is at the heart of Matins.
- *Prime* ("first"): The first of the "Little Hours," Prime is a reading of three psalms following an opening hymn. It's observed at 6 a.m.
- *Lauds* ("praise"): Christians have long seen the parallel between the rising of the sun at dawn and the return of Christ (thus most Catholic and Orthodox churches face east). Lauds is held at dawn, and is focused on the reading of Psalms 148-150 (the "Praise the Lord!" psalms).
- *Terce* ("third"): The second of the "Little Hours," Terce (pronounced "turs") consists of three psalms, the Lord's Prayer, and a hymn. It's observed at 9 a.m.
- *Sext* ("sixth"): The third of the "Little Hours," Sext consists of three psalms, the Lord's Prayer, and a hymn. It's observed at noon.
- *None* ("ninth"): The fourth of the "Little Hours," None (pronounced like "known") consists of three psalms, the Lord's Prayer, and a hymn. It's observed at 3 p.m.
- *Vespers* ("evening"): Held at dusk, Vespers (along with Lauds) is considered one of the two most important Offices of the day. Vespers consists of five psalms, a short Scripture passage, a hymn. It concludes reverently with the singing of the "Magnificat" (Mary's song from Luke 1: 46-55).
- *Compline* ("complete"): The prayers said at night before retiring, Compline (pronounced "cómp-line" or "cómp-lin") is traditionally Psalms 4, 91, and 134 and the "Nunc Dimittis" *(Simeon's Song from Luke 2: 29-32)*.

These are the traditional offices of the Western church as they have been practiced in Roman Catholicism. The prayer book for Anglicans and Episcopalians, *The Book of Common Prayer*, outlines the services of Morning Prayers (a combination of Matins and

Lauds), a noon prayer (compressing the "Little Hours") and Evensong (a combination of Vespers and Compline).

Orthodox Christians practice three offices: *Hesperinos* ("Vespers"; the first office of the day since, like Jews, Orthodox believers start the new day at sunset), *Apodeipnon* (from the Greek, "after supper"; like Compline), and *Orthros* ("dawn").

Theology

As is clear from the preceding history, fixed-hour prayer has been a part of the Christian tradition since its inception. As well as following the psalmist's example to praise God seven times each day, early practitioners were trying to follow Paul's exhortation to "pray without ceasing." As Phyllis Tickle writes:

> To accomplish this, [the Desert Fathers] devised the stratagem of having one group of monks waiting to commence the next office. The result was the introduction into Christian thinking of the concept of a continuous cascade of prayer before the throne of God....Christians today, wherever they practice the discipline of fixed-hour prayer, frequently find themselves filled with a conscious awareness that they are handing their worship, at its final "Amen," on to other Christians in the next time zone.

Tickle makes another important point about the theology and focus of the Office. Whereas many prayers are rightly "petitionary or intercessory or valedictory or any number of other things," fixed-hour prayers always are and always have been exclusively an *offering to God*. Like the sacrifices of the Old Testament, "the Divine Hours are prayers of praise offered as a sacrifice of thanksgiving and faith to God and as a sweet-smelling incense of the human soul before the throne of God."

The Office reorients the one who practices it, turning the gaze from the mundane experiences of daily life on earth, both good and bad, to the One who created it all. Of course, the constant reliance on the psalms throughout the Office inevitably does this. The psalms are cries to God, thanksgivings to God, praises of God—they don't particularly lend themselves to theological reflection, but move the adherent to acknowledge that *we are the creatures and God is the Creator*.

Similarly, the traditional prayers attached to the Office reorient the pray-er. I am always moved by the final prayer for the evening from *The Book of Common Prayer*:

Keep watch, dear Lord, with those who work or watch or weep this night, and give your angels charge over those who sleep. Tend the sick, Lord Christ; give rest to the weary, bless the dying, soothe the suffering, pity the afflicted, shield the joyous; and all for your love's sake. Amen.

No matter what my frame of mind as I head to bed, no matter how well or badly things have gone for me on a given day, when I pray this prayer I'm automatically turned outward, to the needs of others, those I know and those I don't. And I'm reminded that in heaven sits a powerful and sovereign God who has all those who need him in the palm of his hand.

Think of the recent media coverage of faithful Muslims who stop four times a day—at work, at home, while traveling—and pray toward Mecca. This is a countercultural practice: to stop commerce, travel, conversation, even ministry(!). To stop for a short time the advancement of an individual, and by extension society, in order to make an offering to God. Our culture does not reward those of us who stop three or four times per day...but God does. God rewards the one who practices the Office with peace and with an intimacy of relationship that truly is the meaning of life.

practice

Observing the Office is, obviously, a routine that takes an enormous amount of discipline. It's best if the practitioner not begin trying to keep seven Hours a day! From the earliest days, prayer books have reflected a difference between religious (cloistered monks and nuns) and secular (parish priests and nuns) clergy. To be cloistered gives one the opportunity to stop as many times a day as the community determines for prayer; the rest of us don't have that luxury.

When I was on retreat at the Ave Maria Center in Minnesota, we had morning and evening prayers, about half an hour each; at Taizé there are three services per day, each lasting about 45 minutes, around which the whole life of the community revolves. For me, both Taizé and Ave Maria were times of relative cloister, or retreat from the world. Meanwhile other resources take seriously the fact that most of us live in the secular world most of the time and that our daily prayers will be personal and private.

Most prayer books are designed for the public observance of the Daily Office. You might find an Episcopalian, Anglican, Catholic, or Orthodox church near you that has morning and evening prayers. Some downtown churches have a daily noon prayer service for working people. But the fact is, fewer and fewer churches, even of the ancient traditions, are keeping up with daily prayers. Our world is speeding up, people are busy, and, as one recent book has pointed out, worship *is* a "royal *'waste'* of time."

So if you want to experience the Office corporately, that is, with other people, you have two choices: (1) find a monastery or convent nearby where you can join in, or (2) develop a service of your own with a group of people, however small, who are similarly committed to it.

It is likely that most of us will observe the Office privately. To do this, as I said, takes a great deal of discipline. I find that when I travel, I can easily and enthusiastically practice four offices per day: morning, noon, evening, and nighttime. However, when I'm home, it's a lot more difficult to separate myself from Julie and our three young children to go off and pray. Julie and I have experimented some with involving our kids, and I imagine this will be easier as they get older. In the end, each of us must look at our lives and determine, realistically, which Offices we can make a part of our lives.

There's been a recent publishing bonanza of daily prayer books; in addition to the old favorites, the Roman Catholic *Breviary* and the Anglican/Episcopalian *Book of Common Prayer*, there are Benedictine, Celtic, Franciscan, Reformed, and other types available (some of my favorites are in the bibliography). However, I can't imagine that there's a better resource than the three-volume *The Divine Hours* by Phyllis Tickle. She has compiled the best of many other resources, updated the archaic language, and put them in the most usable format imaginable. Using a book like this alleviates much of the frustration that can thwart a novice's attempts at keeping the Office.

final word

Phyllis Tickle, compiler of *The Divine Hours*, writes the following:

> *Asking me why I keep the Offices is like asking me why I go to church. One, granted, is a place of bricks and mortar, but the other is a chapel of the heart, as powerful a place, albeit one of the spirit. The Offices open to me four times a day and call me to remember who owns time and why it is, as a part of creation. All that means really is that four times a day the watchmaker and I have conversation about the clock and my place as a nano-second in it.*

PART III:
VIA ACTIVA:
BODILY APPROACHES
TO SPIRITUALITY

Labyrinth/Body Prayers

Today we walked the labyrinth in community-there are about 70 of us total. Villa Maria has a great labyrinth-it's on the Chartres model, it's quite big, and it has a tree planted in the center. The paths are covered with wood chips and outlined with rocks. I've walked it a couple times since I've been here, but this was the time that the whole group was introduced to it. At first I was jealous of the group experience-that is, I wanted to have the whole labyrinth to myself. Isn't that stupid!?! I felt stupid, so I took my shoes off and walked barefoot so it wouldn't be a totally comfortable experience for me. I used my chockti and found that at the pace I was walking, I completed a circuit of 100 Jesus Prayers and was reciting the Apostles' Creed as I entered the center. I must have walked more quickly on the way out, since I ended with about seven knots left on the rope.

My favorite thing about the labyrinth today was seeing the various postures that people used in the center-kneeling, standing, lying prostrate, arms in the air, arms across the chest (later I found out this is American Sign Language for "love"). Being toward the end of the week, I've gotten to know several of these people and it was cool to see their different prayer postures, and see this embodiment of their prayer relationship with Christ. As with Centering Prayer, I used a yoga position to focus my breathing and my thoughts.

chapter twelve
The Labyrinth

Just as a ship without a helm is driven to and fro by the waves, so a careless man, who abandons his proper course, is tempted in countless ways.

Thomas à Kempis

Jill Kimberly Hartwell Geffrion introduced me to the labyrinth. She has written several books on the subject, including, *Praying the Labyrinth* and *Christian Prayer and Labyrinths*. She has also built several around her family home in Minnesota which she graciously opens to the public. But more importantly, her beautiful spirit and love of the labyrinth, and of God, exudes from her very being. She graciously offers this reflection on one of her experiences:

Pausing at the threshold of the labyrinth, I prayed, "Your will be done." I entered expectantly and began walking on the 14-inch path at a relatively slow pace, savoring the opportunity for my body to connect with God while moving. At about the third turn, I noticed that I'd slowed almost to a stop as I made the 180-degree change in direction.

I have learned that it is always worthwhile to pay attention to what I am noticing as I use a labyrinth. The semicircular stones between my feet reminded me of millstones. This led me to a sense of connectedness with generations of family members who made their living as the power of water turned such stones. Filled with a feeling of my place in history, I continued on. At the next turn, without initially realizing it, I slowed and stopped.

On the labyrinth I often see my life as if I were looking at it in a mirror. My internal and external realities come together in a way that brings new understanding. Since I usually move around turns at the same pace I use on the rest of the path, my sudden desire to stop surprised me. I asked myself and God, *What's going on?* I knew the answer would come in the walking, so I moved on.

I could feel and hear someone coming up behind me on the path. The person was walking more quickly than I. When I got to the next turn I walked straight through it and waited on the far side for him to make the turn and walk on. Once he was past, I moved back on to the half moon shaped slab of stone and stood there in the unexpected awareness, "Here I am again. Stopped at a turn."

"Oh!" I laughed out loud as the realization hit me. "I'm in a time of transition in my life. Many changes (turns) are ahead, including my oldest child's departure for a college 2000 miles away from our home, and my father's impending death. No wonder God is using the turns of this labyrinth to offer me the opportunity to gain needed wisdom about moving through transitions." After that I made at least a brief stop at each of the 28 turns that lead to the center.

As I did so, a fuller understanding came. Being a person who thrives in a crisis, I usually speed up and take care of everything I can in order to make the difficult situation "better." The strategy had worked well, at least I had thought so. Standing on that turn without moving, I realized I was practicing a skill I would need to use often in the coming months. Through this amazing labyrinth pattern that my body was praying, God was communicating this message. "As you enter transitions, you will find it helpful to slow down, perhaps even stop, before entering the experience of change that lies before you."

My labyrinth prayer had once again opened me to the possibility of walking with God, others, and myself in new ways. I had come to the labyrinth with an open mind and heart. God had met me with a gift I had not realized I needed. I moved on, filled with gratitude.

HISTORY

While a labyrinth is technically just a pattern, the type of
labyrinth we are concerned with is laid out on the ground for
walking, and has a circuitous route to a center. Unlike a maze,
there are no wrong turns; the path in is the same as the path out,
as Lauren Artress explains, "Labyrinths are unicursal. They have
one well-defined path that leads us into the center and back out
again. There are no tricks to it, no dead ends or cul-de-sacs, no
intersecting paths." (The origin of the word is hotly debated,
though some believe that *labyrinth* comes from "labrys," the
name of the ancient Minoan double-headed ax, the shape formed
between two back-to-back turns in a Roman-style labyrinth.)

Labyrinths of various shapes and sizes date back thousands
of years: a labyrinthine rock carving in Sardinia dates to around
2500 B.C.; pottery from 1300 B.C. in Syria shows a labyrinth;
a clay tablet in Greece from 1200 B.C. shows the design; and
the remains of a labyrinth from around the same time have been
found at the top of Mt. Knossos, on the isle of Crete (especially
interesting because legend has it that the ancient Trojans were
remnants of the tribe of Benjamin, exiled after the rape and mur-
der of the Levite's concubine as told in Judges 19-20).

Labyrinthine designs have been a part of almost every culture
and religion, and they were incorporated into Christian art and
architecture in the first centuries after Jesus. The earliest extant
Christian labyrinth dates from 325 at a church in Algiers; at its
center is a mosaic acrostic spelling *santa ecclesia*, "holy church."

In the Middle Ages, when pilgrimages to Jerusalem, Rome,
and Santiago were becoming more dangerous because of the Crusades, the church ordained seven cathedrals in France as alter-
nate pilgrimage sites. One of these was the cathedral at Chartres,
the location of the most well-preserved labyrinth from that time.
Although no literature mentioning the labyrinth from that period
remains, it seems that to complete the pilgrimage to Chartres, a
pilgrim would walk the route to the center of the labyrinth, which
is laid out in the floor, before proceeding to the altar to receive the
Eucharist.

Because of its size, its beautifully symmetrical layout, and
its importance in Christian history, the Chartres labyrinth has
become the archetype for thousands of more recently constructed
labyrinths. Laid in the floor between 1194 and 1220, the labyrinth
at Chartres is of the 11-circuit design. That means 11 concentric

circles surround the center circle, and the path meanders between the circuits. When seen from above, the turns, 10 of which form labryses, create four quadrants and a cruciform design. The path turns seven times in each quadrant and six times along the entrance or exit path. The exterior of the labyrinth has 113 notches, or "lunations," which some believe form a lunar calendar used to set the date of Easter. The entire pattern is 42 feet in diameter.

At the center of the labyrinth is a circle outlined by six smaller circles. Some see in this a six-petaled flower, the rose being a symbol both of the Virgin Mary and of the Holy Spirit. The six petals can be understood to represent the six days of creation, and some walkers visit each petal, thanking God for what was created on each day. Others see seven circles (the six smaller and the one larger that binds them) as the intersection of heaven (the Trinity) and earth (the four directions).

In 1991, Lauren Artress, a pastor at Grace Episcopal Cathedral in San Francisco, went to Chartres to walk the labyrinth there — she had walked another labyrinth and was interested in introducing one in her own church. When she and her friends arrived, the medieval labyrinth was covered with chairs. Artress and her friends moved the chairs and, before they were told to put them back, had a chance to walk the 861-foot path to the center.

Artress was deeply moved by the experience. Upon her return to San Francisco, her church painted an 11-circuit labyrinth on canvas for use at Grace Cathedral. The response was overwhelming. People lined up around the block for the semi-monthly walkings. Veriditas: The World-Wide Labyrinth Project, the organization she founded, was soon receiving requests from around the country to speak, write, and lead retreats that include labyrinth walking. Concurrently, there has been a massive revival of labyrinth construction, sales, and training since the early 1990s. Every major city in North America now boasts numerous labyrinths, churches of every persuasion have incorporated them into worship, and institutions like hospitals and seminaries have integrated them into their gardens.

An almost forgotten ancient and medieval spiritual tool is now arguably one of the most popular experiential devices in Christian spirituality.

Theology

More is being written about the labyrinth every year, though at this time there exists no full-length study on the Christian

theology of the labyrinth. Still, there is much about the practice
of walking the labyrinth that lends itself to deepening the faith
journey.

The labyrinth is a metaphor for life. The Christian life is often
described as a pilgrimage of the faithful who are in but not of the
world. We progress down a path that's laid out by God—even
though we rarely foresee its twists and turns—toward the even-
tual goal of unity with Christ.

The labyrinth thus replicates our spiritual journey. We enter
and follow a path, not knowing where it will take us, but knowing we will eventually arrive at the center. Sometimes the path
leads inward toward the ultimate goal, only to lead back outwards
again. We meet others along the path—some we meet face-to-face
stepping aside to let them pass; some catch up to us from behind
and pass us; others we pass along the way. At the center we rest,
watch others, pray. Sometimes we stay in the center a long time;
other times we leave quickly.

The point is, the labyrinth is a walking prayer:

*The labyrinth is an archetype, a rich symbol that reaches into the depths of
our human experience and hints at meaning that is both inescapable and
inexhaustible. As a circle, it is a universal symbol of unity and wholeness. The
labyrinth invites us to a journey within the sacred circle itself, offering a glimpse
of the ineffable mystery of God.*

Much has been written about the "sacred geometry" of labyrinth designs, most of which isn't particularly relevant for our
purposes. There is, however, an inward-outward movement that
also reflects the Christian life. Gordon Mursell notes, "The walk
inward becomes a journey of purification, meditation in the centre
is compared to illumination, and the journey outward becomes
union, a return to service in the world for the walking meditator
who is refreshed and healed."

practice

St. Augustine once said that some problems can be "solved
by walking" and the labyrinth is a tool to help facilitate this
perambulatory prayer. Since virtually no literature exists
explaining how medieval Christians used the labyrinth in their
lives, all instruction on labyrinth use is recent and evolving. Jill
Geffrion writes, "Two truths about labyrinth praying guided
me through my pilgrimage and opened the door to many rich

experiences. The first was a deep, intuitional knowing that there was no 'right' way to pray the labyrinth. The other was that God is very present in the midst of labyrinth praying."

One of the most common ways to pray the labyrinth is to ask God a question upon entering and then to listen for an answer. Another method is to pray for yourself on the way in, stop and simply experience God's love in the center, and pray for others on the way out (or vice versa). One of the first times I walked a labyrinth, I asked God what I needed to hear; by the time I was in the center, I was convicted that I needed to spend more time praying for those around me, and I spent the way out doing just that.

It can also be meaningful to recite the Lord's Prayer, liturgical prayers, or psalms while walking. As Judy Cannato writes of her initial labyrinth experience:

> It was during this first walk that I began to reflect on Psalm 139. Walking the labyrinth felt like walking around in the shoes of the psalmist who sang of the One who searches our hearts and knows us better than we know ourselves. The labyrinth enabled me to be immersed in the psalm, while the psalm rendered the labyrinth a deeply moving experience of prayer.

Finding a labyrinth is becoming much easier than it was even a few years ago. Grace Cathedral hosts a worldwide labyrinth locator on its website (*http://wwll.veriditas.labyrinthsociety.org*) and many local newspapers have done stories highlighting the labyrinths in their vicinity. Most outdoor labyrinths are open all the time, while indoor labyrinths usually have posted hours. It's also possible to purchase a canvas labyrinth, to order instructions for making one, or even to print a page-sized labyrinth off of a website and "walk" with your finger (google "finger labyrinth" to find one).

A whole different kind of labyrinth has been pioneered by Jonny Baker and the Youth for Christ staff in London. Baker's interactive, multimedia labyrinth has 11 stations. Individuals are given a CD player and headphones, and a voice leads the pray-er through the stations with narration that is recorded over ambient music.

The first five stations on the path are journey inward, noise, letting go, hurts, and distractions. At the center is "Holy Space," where the pray-er is told, "Let God love you." On the way out, the stations are outward journey, self, planet, others, and impressions. The stations incorporate computers, televisions, and artwork to complete the multisensory experience. You can "virtually" experience this Labyrinth Project on the web (*www.labyrinth. org.uk*).

When visiting a public labyrinth, be respectful of the people who have opened the labyrinth and of the others who might be walking it when you visit. Remember, you have the *option* of walking—some people have a powerful experience sitting along the edge and watching others walk. Don't take pictures or video unless you've gotten permission. And allow yourself as much time as you need to complete the journey.

A final word

In her book, *Exploring the Labyrinth*, Melissa Gayle West writes of the simplicity of the labyrinth's single path:

> *Since the destination is assured, there are no obstacles to overcome, no muddles to figure out, no dead ends to retrace. What remains for the labyrinth walker is simply the deeply meditative and symbolic discipline of setting one foot in front of the other, of honoring the journey itself and what it has to teach. The mind can be stilled and attention paid to the body, the wisdom of the heart, and the graces of being rather than doing.*

Centering Prayer

This was tough. I've never tried centering prayer before, and I really didn't even know what it was. I guess I'd sum it up as being about (1) the present, and (2) God's love. We weren't given too much instruction, just to sit or stand or lie still for 45 minutes, to control our breath, and to use a name or image for God repetitively. We were taken on a guided meditation in which we met up with Jesus on a road and sat with him on a bench to talk. It was very cool, and I really got stuck on the moment when Jesus and I met on the road—I suddenly became a little boy, maybe 8 years old, and I threw my arms around Jesus' waist and buried my head in his robe. And I was hanging on to him for dear life—I don't think we ever made it to the bench to talk!

When it came time to center, I felt like I should focus on the phrase, "Good Shepherd". Breathe in, "Good," breathe out, "Shepherd." The first 15 minutes were a bust—the woman next to me fell asleep and was snoring, and I was lying down. So I stood up and moved to another place in the room. I decided to use the standing mountain position, the first pose in Ashtanga Yoga: feet together, toes pointed up, butt clenched, spine long, and shoulders down and back.

It is embarrassing to admit how much my mind wandered, especially to future things, just as they told us it would. I constantly found myself somewhere else, and I had to bring myself back to "Good Shepherd"—even though I never stopped repeating the phrase, I still wandered.

BUT, something very cool did happen—I got into it enough to lose track of time. I was disciplined enough not to look at the clock, not even to open my eyes at the beginning when I was tempted to. That temptation passed and I must have gotten centered, because I wasn't expecting it or ready for it when the leader said, "Amen," at the end. That was cool!

chapter thirteen
stations of the cross

If you cannot contemplate high and heavenly things,
take refuge in the Passion of Christ, and love to dwell
within his Sacred Wounds. For if you devoutly seek the
Wounds of Jesus and the precious marks of his Passion,
you will find great strength in all troubles.

Thomas à Kempis

I've had the good fortune of walking the Stations (often called "making the Stations") in many beautiful and profound places: St. Peter's Basilica in Rome, in the gardens of Taizé in France, at a monastery in San Antonio. I've seen them acted out on stage, and I've walked through the "living" Stations. I even have a setting of the stations on my handheld PC, so I often make the Stations while I'm on a plane.

But my most profound experience with the Stations took place in the gym of my church in Minnesota. A group of junior high boys had asked their Bible study leader, Tim, about the Stations—they'd heard about them from their

Catholic friends. So one afternoon, Tim took about six of these boys to downtown Minneapolis, and they went in to the beautiful Basilica of St. Mary and poked around. Not knowing any prayers to say — or even how to make out the Roman numerals — the boys wandered around the ancient-feeling space, transfixed by the mystery before them.

It wasn't long before those boys and their friends were asking for something like that in our church. At the time, neither Tim nor I knew much about the Stations, so it took some research to pull it off. We searched the Internet for pictures of the Stations, and we asked our friend Sherry to print them on large pieces of tagboard and laminate them. Then Tim wrote out a brief explanation of each station and an accompanying prayer, and Sherry laminated those as well.

On the appointed night, we darkened the gym and posted the Stations in order around the walls. Under each Station we placed five or six votive candles. We set up a small stereo in one corner and played some CDs of medieval chants. Tim invited the 50 or 60 junior highers who showed up that night to walk the Stations, either alone or in pairs. They could take as much time as they wanted, he only asked that they respect those around them as they walked.

As might be expected with early teens, there was some giggling, and some of the kids almost jogged around the circuit. But for the majority, the response was overwhelming: they loved it! Many of these 12- and 13-year-olds who had been hearing about Jesus for years in Sunday school felt like they really experienced his suffering for the first time. Several of them reported that they finally *got* what Jesus went through.

For me personally, the greatest thing about the Stations is that every time I journey through them, I am reminded of this and many other poignant experiences I've had with the Stations. It's as if each time I walk them, I'm also walking with my past. There is a familiarity that is bred by walking the Stations, no matter if I'm on a plane to Newark or in the seat of Vatican City.

That, I suppose, is the beauty of the Stations — that the suffering of Jesus unites me with all others — past, present, and future — who have endeavored to follow him all the way to the Cross. And it also unites me with me, with every time I've made the Stations, when I've been flying high and when I've been in the depths of despair. It even unites me with my future, for the Stations will surely be a part of me into eternity.

History

From the earliest days of the church, Christians have journeyed to Jerusalem to retrace the path Jesus took as he carried his cross from Pilate's house to Golgotha. According to tradition, this path, which has become known as the *Via Dolorosa* ("Way of Sorrow") and the *Via Crucis* ("Way of the Cross"), was walked often by Jesus' mother, Mary, after his death. St. Jerome (ca.325-420), known primarily for translating the Bible into Latin, wrote of the hundreds of pilgrims in Jerusalem who walked this devotional path in his day.

The route Jesus walked quickly became well known, and informal markers pointed out the places he started, received his cross, where he stopped and fell, met his mother, and was assisted by Simon of Cyrene. Pilgrims then arrived at the hill known as the "Place of the Skull" where Jesus was stripped of his garments and crucified. By the Middle Ages, visitors to Jerusalem were taken on this *Via Sacra* ("Sacred Way") by guides. And in other cities around Europe, facsimiles of the *Via Sacra* were developed so that pilgrims could walk this journey with Jesus more than once in a lifetime. One of the first of these was in Bologna, Italy, where a collection of chapels was built to replicate the important pilgrimage sites in Jerusalem.

In 1342, the holy places in Jerusalem were placed under the guardianship of the Franciscan Order. A fifteenth century English pilgrim, William Wey, was the first to write about the practice of stopping, praying and meditating on Jesus' journey to crucifixion. By the turn of the sixteenth century, replicas of the *Via Dolorosa* had been constructed all over Italy, Spain, and Germany, many replicating the exact route in Jerusalem down to the measured-off paces between the stopping points.

The early literature has no set number of stations; they vary from 7 to 37. By the seventeenth century, the most common number of stations was 14; but at the time, Jerusalem was in the hands of the Turks, who had made it illegal to stop along the route, uncover one's head, and pray. So it seems most likely that the 14 stations we now know were formalized around Europe instead of in Jerusalem. In the late seventeenth century, the Roman Catholic Church connected indulgences to the practice of praying the Stations, making the Stations very popular. While that connection went by the wayside during the Reformation, it remains the case that, to this day, almost every Catholic sanctuary has the

14 stations around the walls. Very recently, some churches have added a fifteenth station, celebrating Christ's resurrection, but all agree that this station is not to be observed during Lent.

Unlike many of the other practices I've discussed, this one lends itself to some customization. The Stations are most often practiced during Lent and especially during Holy Week; many churches hold special Good Friday services that center around the Stations. Other churches leave the Stations up year-round. The set-up of the Stations varies from place to place as well. The most famous set of Stations outside of Jerusalem may be around the Colosseum in Rome; every Friday a Franciscan Friar leads pilgrims through these Stations, and on Good Friday, the Pope walks them. Some of the artwork connected with the Stations is world renowned, but most churches simply have 14 crosses on the walls, each with a Roman numeral over the top signifying the station. Since no prescribed prayer is attached to the practice of the Stations, beautiful prayers for each Station abound in prayer books, on websites, and in Catholic and Protestant liturgies.

Theology

"If any want to be my followers, let them deny themselves and take up their cross and follow me." In no uncertain terms Jesus makes his claim on our lives in the Gospels. We are to follow him to the cross and to follow him on the *Via Crucis*, the way of the cross. Jesus' entire life, and especially his three-year ministry can be seen as part of this road, for every miracle he performed, every parable he told, and every invective he unleashed on the Pharisees took him one step closer to his crucifixion.

When he entered Jerusalem on Palm Sunday, the segment of that road he traveled was paved with cloaks and tree branches. By Friday of that week, the same stones were spattered with drops of blood from his forehead. Shuffled between Pilate and Herod that morning, Luke records the beginning of Jesus' march to the cross:

> So Pilate decided to grant their demand. He released the man who had been thrown into prison for insurrection and murder, the one they asked for, and surrendered Jesus to their will. As they led him away, they seized Simon from Cyrene, who was on his way in from the country, and put the cross on him and made him carry it behind Jesus. A large number of people followed him, including women who mourned and wailed for him. Jesus turned and said to

them, "Daughters of Jerusalem, do not weep for me; weep for yourselves and
for your children."

The 14 Stations of the Cross trace Jesus' path from Pilate's
house to Golgotha to his tomb, mixing some events that we
find in Scripture with some that come to us via the tradition of
the church. Cardinal John Henry Newman (1801-1890) was a
renowned churchman who wrote short and long reflections on
the Stations. Here are devotions that I've written for the Stations,
which are inspired by and indebted to Newman's:

You are about to walk along the Way of the Cross, also called the
Via Dolorosa or the Road of Sorrow. The Way of the Cross traces
the journey taken by Jesus on the last day of his earthly life. Over
15 stations, you will travel with Jesus from the moment he was
condemned to death to the victorious moment of his resurrection.
This path has been walked by millions of Christians over 2000 years.
May God bless you on your journey.

station one: jesus is condemned to death

The holy, just, and true Son of God was judged by sinners and
sentenced to die. Judas betrayed him, the crowd shouted for his
death, and Pilate sentenced him. In beginning this road to the cross,
Jesus becomes one with everyone who has ever suffered, everyone
who has ever bled or been scorned or been unfairly punished. He
becomes one with you and me. The very Creator of the universe
experiences the ultimate human suffering.

O Lord, may I be moved by this journey. May I make this journey with you
and you with me. Do not leave me alone on this way, even though your own
followers abandoned you at your hour of need. We adore you, O Christ, and we
bless you because by your holy cross you have redeemed the world. Amen.

station two: jesus receives his cross

Jesus carries the weight of his own cross on his shoulders, and upon
that cross is heaped the weight of all of our sins. My sins cost him this
humiliation. He became a human being so he could enter into our joy
and our pain, and so, ultimately, he could take our sins away. And
now the weight of those sins crushes down on him with every step.

O Lord God Almighty, you bear the weight of the whole world—you bore the weight of all my sins, and, though they wearied you, you carried them all the way to your death. We adore you, O Christ, and we bless you because by your holy cross you have redeemed the world. Amen.

station Three: jesus falls under the weight of the cross for the first Time

Suddenly, Jesus falls. The weight of the cross is too much. He cannot bear it. He is on the ground, and he knows what it is to feel defeated, weak, unable to go on. And yet, he must go on. The soldiers pick him up and force him to continue.

O dear Lord, by this your first fall raise me out of sin, I who have so miserably fallen under its power. Give me strength to continue my journey, even when I feel that I can't go on. We adore you, O Christ, and we bless you because by your holy cross you have redeemed the world. Amen.

station Four: jesus meets His mother

What must it be like to see your mother as you are walking to your own execution? Mary gave birth to this boy, she brought him as an infant into the temple, she lifted him up in her arms when the wise men came to adore him. She fled with him to Egypt, she took him up to Jerusalem when he was twelve years old. He lived with her at Nazareth for 30 years. She was with him at the marriage feast. Even when he had left her to preach, she hovered about him. And now she's there to give him comfort at the hour of his death.

Dear Jesus, what did you think when you saw your mother there? Give me the steadfast faith she had, and the courage to stay by your side, even when all others have fled. We adore you, O Christ, and we bless you because by your holy cross you have redeemed the world. Amen.

station Five: simon of cyrene Helps jesus to carry the cross

Jesus could have carried the cross alone, but he allowed a man named Simon to help him. Just as he could feed the hungry and clothe the naked and build homes for the homeless without me…but he does not. Instead, he relies on me to aid him, to help him build the kingdom, to help him carry the cross.

Dear Lord, teach me to suffer with you, make it pleasant for me to suffer for your sake. And when my time comes to help you bear the cross, give me the courage and strength of Simon to step forward and do my part. We adore you, O Christ, and we bless you because by your holy cross you have redeemed the world. Amen.

station six: The face of jesus is wiped by veronica

As Jesus walks this sorrowful journey, the blood that drips from the crown of thorns on his head mixes with the spit of those who mock him. Out of the crowd comes a compassionate friend, Veronica, who wipes the spit, blood, and sweat from his face. Only for a moment, Jesus feels some relief.

O Lord God, Veronica is an example of someone who does the simple, compassionate act in a time of need. Remind me that it's not always the big things that matter, but often the smallest that can have an impact. We adore you, O Christ, and we bless you because by your holy cross you have redeemed the world. Amen.

station seven: jesus falls a second time.

The weight is too much and Jesus falls again. His knees scrape on the road, and his face is pushed into the dirt. Maybe he's reminded that "from dust you came and to dust you shall return." Maybe he catches his breath for a moment before the soldiers force him back to his feet.

King of the Universe, you tasted the dirt as the heavy wood of the cross fell on top of you. I am again shocked at the weight of my own sin, and I am humbled that you would suffer such humiliation for me. We adore you, O Christ, and we bless you because by your holy cross you have redeemed the world. Amen.

station eight: The women of jerusalem mourn for our lord

Jesus broke so many barriers for his day: he touched lepers, he healed on the Sabbath, and he spoke to women in public. Jesus ignored traditions that were oppressive, and he stood up to the authorities who challenged him. And now the women of Jerusalem show their gratitude by meeting Jesus along the way and crying over his fate.

Earlier, Jesus prophesied that the women of Jerusalem would weep for him, and now that prophecy is fulfilled.

> *O Jesus, the cross is so commonplace in our world: around necks, hanging on walls, in cemeteries. Remind me what an awful torture you had to endure, so that I, too, might weep over your death when I see a cross. We adore you, O Christ, and we bless you because by your holy cross you have redeemed the world. Amen.*

station Nine: Jesus falls the third time

Utterly broken and devastated, Jesus falls again. This time, even the soldiers know he can't rise by his own power. They roughly grab the Son of God and half-drag, half-push him up the rest of the hill. Is the cross getting heavier? Is Jesus getting weaker? The life that has raised the dead, healed the lame, and given sight to the blind is draining from him.

> *O Jesus, only-begotten Son of God, the Word made flesh, I adore with fear and trembling and deep thankfulness your awful humiliation. The fact that you allowed yourself to be so disgraced brings me to my knees. We adore you, O Christ, and we bless you because by your holy cross you have redeemed the world. Amen.*

station Ten: Jesus is stripped of His garments.

Jesus' life was a life of poverty — he gave up all earthly possessions to preach the gospel of Good News. Now, even the cloak he wears is violently stripped from him, tearing open the whip wounds on his back. As if the indignity of crucifixion weren't enough, Jesus now stands naked before the crowd.

> *Lord Jesus, you withstood the mocking and derision heaped upon you, and you faced your fate with dignity. May I, too, stand with courage when all is stripped from me. We adore you, O Christ, and we bless you because by your holy cross you have redeemed the world. Amen.*

station Eleven: Jesus is Nailed to the cross

Huge, sharp spikes are hammered through Jesus' wrists and feet — he nearly loses consciousness with each swing of the hammer. Now he is raised up and the cross drops with a thud into a hole in the ground.

Jesus' weight hangs on those spikes, and to breathe he has to pull himself up on the nails. A sponge with vinegar is stuck in his mouth, and soldiers below him gamble for his clothes, even as the blood, breath, and life drain from his body.

O Jesus, dear Jesus, though you never sinned, you hang there on the cross. I should be there, not you. You hang there in my place. We adore you, O Christ, and we bless you because by your holy cross you have redeemed the world. Amen.

station twelve: jesus dies upon the cross

Every breath is a struggle. Wheezing, Jesus whispers in a voice barely audible, "Father, into your hands I commend my spirit." One more gasping breath, then his head drops, and it is finished. A soldier jams a spear between his ribs as a test, and the blood and water that issue forth show conclusively that the Savior of the world is indeed dead. The price is paid, and we are redeemed.

Father in Heaven, what did you feel as your Son died upon that cruel piece of wood? Holy Spirit, did you grieve when your Divine Brother was taken from you? We adore you, O Christ, and we bless you because by your holy cross you have redeemed the world. Amen.

station thirteen: jesus is laid in the arms of his mother

Jesus hasn't been held in his mother's arms since he was a baby, but now his lifeless body is taken down from the cross and laid across her lap. What tears she cries! Her 33-year-old son, the Messiah, crusted with blood, naked, and dead is beyond her help, so she, too, is helpless.

Father God, did you weep to see the once naïve, teenage girl now three decades later hold the dead body of her son...of your Son? We adore you, O Christ, and we bless you because by your holy cross you have redeemed the world. Amen.

station fourteen: jesus is laid in the tomb

At the very moment that Jesus was closest to his eternal glory, he seemed to be farthest from it. His body was placed in a stone-cold tomb, sealed with a massive rock, guarded by Roman soldiers. Death is so very final.

Give me the trust, O Christ, that your plans are higher than mine. For even when all seems lost, you're still at work. Death is not the final word for you, Son of Life. We adore you, O Christ, and we bless you because by your holy cross you have redeemed the world. Amen.

station fifteen: the tomb is empty

Sunday morning — Easter. The stone is rolled away, the tomb is empty except for some burial clothes. First the women find it this way, and soon after the disciples come to investigate. It truly is empty. The word goes forth: He is risen! He is risen, indeed! Death could not win, the tomb does not have the victory. Jesus Christ is stronger even than death!

My heart rejoices, Jesus, that the tomb could not hold you. You burst forth with new life, and you give me new life. I accept the gift you've given me — help me never to take it for granted! We adore you, O Christ, and we bless you because by your holy cross you have redeemed the world! Amen.

You have now walked with Jesus from Pilate's house, along the Via Dolorosa, to the top of Mt. Calvary. You have seen him crucified, dead, and laid in a tomb. And, finally, you have visited his empty tomb, so you know that his victory is complete. Now what? Will it change you? Will you respond to this ultimate gift given on your behalf?

That's up to you. Whatever you choose, may God bless you on your journey. He loves you more than you could ever imagine.

Peace.

Making the Stations has never been an intellectual exercise, but a spiritual and emotional pursuit. Nor is it merely an historical act, as we see in Henri Nouwen's prayer for the Stations:

Dear Jesus,

You once were condemned; you are still being condemned. You once carried your cross; you are still carrying your cross. You once died; you are dying still. You once rose from the dead; you are still rising from the dead.

At his Last Supper, Jesus washed his disciples' feet and, presumably talking about his entire life and ministry, said, "I have set an example that you should do as I have done to you." To pray the Stations is to follow that example, meditating on the suffering that Jesus experienced, the suffering we encounter, and the suffering throughout the world.

practice

The most common way to practice the Stations is to go to a church that has them around the walls; most Roman Catholic churches have the Stations, and many monasteries have them outdoors along a prayer path.

Many churches host a "Living Stations of the Cross" during Holy Week. In the Living Stations, participants gather in small groups. After an introduction by their host, they are led from station to station. At each station, a responsive liturgy is read while actors stand still in a montage of the particular scene. Between stations, the group sings a meditative chorus (Taizé songs work well for this).

Here are three examples from a retreat called Cursillo (there are seven stations in this setting):

introduction

Leader: Paul said that we who have been baptized into Jesus have been joined to his suffering and his death and his resurrection. As we make these Stations of the Cross, the steps along the path Jesus took from his conviction to his crucifixion, know that each of us makes this journey with him. Let us pray:

People: Lord Jesus, the curtain is now about to go up on the awful drama of your love—a drama which we cannot forget, a drama of a love that will not forget us. And as we hear your words, "Take up your cross daily and follow me," some of us shudder to let those words come too close, lest the burden be too great and its shame too bitter. If we could only see that your command to follow you to Calvary is not just an iron law of cruel fate, but a condition of everlasting happiness—maybe then we could better make the journey.

Christ Speaks: These steps you are now about to pass through, you do not take alone. I walk with you. Though you are you and I am I, yet we are truly one—one in Christ. You, my brother, my sister, were baptized into me, joined to me, marked with the cross of Christ forever! And therefore my Way of the Cross two thousand years ago and your "way" now are also one. But note this difference: my life was incomplete until it was crowned by my death—your journey will only be complete when you have let me crown it with my life!

second station: jesus takes up his cross

Christ Speaks: This cross, this chunk of tree—this is what my Father chose for me. The crosses you bear are largely the products of your daily lives, are they not? And yet my Father chose them for you, too. Receive them from his hands. Take heart, my brother, my sister: I will not let your burdens grow one ounce too heavy for your strength.

People: We know, Lord, how crosses are made. Your will is the timber that points up; ours is the one which crosses it. When we place our will against yours, we make the cross. Grant that we may make no more crosses for you, but that we might place our will alongside yours to make a yoke that will always be a burden fit to carry. Amen.

fourth station: simon helps jesus

Christ Speaks: My strength is gone—I can no longer bear the cross alone. And so the soldiers make Simon give me aid. This Simon is like you, my brother, my sister. Give me your strength. Each time you lift some burden from someone's back, you lift as with your very hand the awful weight of the cross which crushes me.

People: Lord, help me to realize that every time I wipe a dish, pick up an object off the floor, assist another in some small task, or give someone preference in traffic or at the store—each time I feed the hungry, clothe the naked, teach the ignorant, or lend my hand in any way—it matters not to whom, my name is Simon. And the kindness I extend to them, I really give to you. Amen.

Another form of the Living Stations takes place on a stage or at the front of a sanctuary. Again, actors pose in the position of the scene and a responsive reading is read. Between scenes, the sanctuary is darkened and a song is chanted, or silence is kept.

A final word
Thomas Merton, possibly the most celebrated monk of the twentieth century, wrote this about the eve of his decision to enter the monastery:

The Retreat Master, in one of his conferences, told us a long story of a man who had once come to Gethsemani [Abbey], and who had not been able to make up his mind to become a monk, and had fought and prayed about it for days. Finally, went the story, he had made the Stations of the Cross, and at the final station had prayed fervently to be allowed the grace of dying in the Order.

"You know," said the Retreat Master, "they say that no petition you ask at the 14th station is ever refused."

In any case, this man finished his prayer, and went back to his room and in an hour or so he collapsed, and they just had time to receive his request for admission to the Order when he died.

He lies buried in the monks' cemetery, in the oblate's habit.

And so, the last thing I did before leaving Gethsemani, was to do the Stations of the Cross, and to ask, with my heart in my throat, at the 14th station, for the grace of a vocation to the Trappists, if it were pleasing to God.

Centering Prayer

I had the strangest experience today—I was in Centering Prayer and really emptying my mind, using the word "love" to rebuff every thought. Then, out of nowhere, the planes flew into the World Trade Center in my mind. It was a very strong image, a picture, which is different since it's usually words that I battle, not pictures. But the weirdest thing of all was my preordained response to that image: "Love." Weird, but also highly appropriate, I guess.

chapter fourteen
pilgrimage

*Keep yourself a stranger and pilgrim upon this earth,
to whom the affairs of this world are of no concern. Keep
your heart free and lifted up to God, for here you have no
abiding city.*

Thomas à Kempis

Blair Bertrand is a Presbyterian pastor in
Canada. In the summer of 2003, he and a
friend traversed the ancient pilgrimage route
to Santiago in Spain. Here he writes about
the thrill of arriving at his destination after a
month of hiking:

For anyone but a pilgrim to Santiago de Compostela, it is a strange photograph to cherish but
cherish it I do. Lost amid the eclectic cityscape
of twenty-first century Spain is a glimpse of a
thirteenth century cathedral. For anyone but a
pilgrim, the Picture is a jumbled street scene, not
well framed and definitely lacking in any artistic
merit. For me, the first view of that steeple meant
the end of a 30-day spiritual odyssey.

My pilgrimage partner, Peter, and I had planned our journey for
months, trained for weeks, and complained for at least the last two
thirds of the trek. Still, I met the end with mixed feelings. On one
hand I was happy to stop walking, to finally slough off my pack and
not need to pick it up again, to have my feet stop pulsating at the end
of the day. Those were the immediate feelings of relief.

Mixed in with these sighs of relief, however, were pangs of sorrow —
the sadness of losing the beautiful routine of walking contemplation,
of saying goodbye to my fellow pilgrims, of returning to a life that was
dictated by my watch rather than the rhythms of the path.

These mixed feelings reveal that pilgrimage, at least for me, is both
timeless and very immediate. While I walked through archways
made hundreds of years ago and took part in a tradition that has been
carried out for thousands of years, there was no escaping that my
legs ached right then and there. Peter and I often helped our fellow pilgrims with their ill-fitting equipment and the blisters that resulted from
their lack of preparation. There is nothing less mystical than smelly
feet, so I was continually reminded that pilgrimage isn't all about
other-worldly spirituality--it is rooted in the here and now. At the
same time, contemplating the Psalms, talking with my fellow pilgrims,
visiting Gothic cathedrals, and seeing the natural beauty of Spain all
pointed to a reality greater than what sits in front of me each day.

We were going to a place where we would celebrate with all of the
friends and companions we had met along the way, and there was a
real sense of accomplishment when we reached the end. Meanwhile,
all along the route there were markers that pointed beyond this time.
We were in some sense journeying towards God and God's kingdom.
Our times of fellowship foreshadowed a final fellowship with God.
Our times of prayer and contemplation were a foretaste of worshipping forever in God's presence. Our satisfaction at the end of a hard
day, a premonition of the satisfaction of knowing that we had faith-
fully run the race set before us. In this mingling I felt God's presence,
I think because I felt present to God.

For others, the picture of a cathedral you can hardly make out holds
no value; for me, the picture points to the greater reality of God and
the pilgrimage of life that all Christians embark on when they accept
Christ's invitation to "Come, follow me."

History

The Bible is replete with archetypes for pilgrimage: Abram and Sarai left their homeland at God's command; Moses and the Israelites wandered for 40 years, following God toward their promised homeland; Jesus was, in many ways, a pilgrim during his entire three-year ministry, constantly moving from place to place; Paul undertook three missionary journeys to far-off lands, and other apostles followed his example. Indeed, as we'll explore in the Theology section below, all of life east of Eden can be considered a pilgrimage.

And, as the New Testament states repeatedly, followers of Christ are "strangers and pilgrims on the earth." *Pilgrim* comes from the Latin word for "resident alien", and it can also mean "to wander over a great distance." Pilgrimage thus reflects both of those senses: wandering and distance. Though the wandering is not aimless—it's pointed toward a goal—the wanderer spends a majority of the journey in a foreign land. And the greater the distance the more admirable the journey.

The Roman Emperor Constantine converted to Christianity and made it a legal religion in the Empire in 313. In 326, his mother Helena—later canonized—made a famous pilgrimage to Jerusalem. There she gathered dozens of sacred relics, most notably the cross on which Jesus was crucified, and brought them back to Rome. Within two years, the fame of her journey spread, and pilgrims were setting off from all over Italy to visit the Holy Land.

The first guidebooks for such pilgrims were composed in the same century, and they record much information both about the journey and about the traditions of Christian worship in Jerusalem at the time. The most famous and most complete of these is the *Peregrinatio Egeriae*, (the *Pilgrimage of Egeria*), which was written in 385 and discovered in Italy in 1884. Egeria seems to have been a nun or abbess who over three years visited all of the major biblical sites in the Holy Land, recording in detail what she saw.

Jerusalem was, and still remains, the primary pilgrimage site for Christians. Soon after Constantine's decree, churches were built over many of the sacred spots from Jesus' life and passion. Egeria describes visits to many of these spots during Holy Week, and her descriptions seem to show the beginnings of the Stations of the Cross.

Next in the hierarchy of pilgrimage sites was Rome, being the burial spot of the preeminent apostles, Peter and Paul. Constantine commissioned basilicas to be built over each of their tombs, and both structures had to be enlarged frequently to accommodate the crushing number of pilgrims.

In the early Middle Ages, Santiago de Compostela in Spain began to rise to prominence; between the eleventh and thirteenth centuries it was by far the most popular of pilgrimage destinations. Tradition held that, before he was beheaded in Jerusalem in A.D. 44, the Apostle James the Greater (brother of John, Son of Thunder) went on a missionary journey to Spain. Further, popular belief held that his remains returned to Spain, either miraculously or brought by a king, and were interred in Santiago (Spanish for 'Saint James'). An enormous cathedral was built over James' purported burial spot, and thousands upon thousands of pilgrims visited the shrine.

Pilgrims to Santiago and other shrines were distinguished by their garb: in addition to sturdy shoes and a deerskin coat, all pilgrims carried a staff (*bordón*) and a bag (*escarcela*) and wore a patch. The staff was four to five feet long with an iron tip at one end and was useful for fighting off wild animals and for balancing through tricky river and mountain crossings. But, more importantly, "it was credited with chasing the devil away, and it stood for the *lignum crucis*, the Wood of the Cross." The bag was a trapezoid-shaped deerskin satchel, wider at the base than the top. "The *escarcela* had to be narrow and flat to remind the pilgrim to rely on the Great Provider alone instead of on his own provisions, it had to be always open in order to give and receive, and it had to be made of animal skin to evoke the mortifications of the flesh."

The patch served a dual purpose. First of all, it (supposedly) granted the pilgrim safe passage through all lands by the authority of the church, though pilgrimages were always very dangerous. And the specific patch denoted the pilgrim's destination: two crossed palm leaves for Jerusalem, two keys (as given to St. Peter) for Rome, and a scallop shell for Santiago (the shell represents the open hand of one who freely gives and receives, and victorious pilgrims collected shells to bring home from the beach outside Santiago). So important were these items that many exhumed medieval graves hold their denizens along with a staff and scallop shells. Many of these items would be given to the pilgrim by her parish church before she set off on her journey.

The pilgrimage was an arduous journey. For one who lived in France, the round trip to Santiago, for example, took about six months, and it was close to a year's journey for someone from northern Germany. The trail was pocked with treacherous mountain passes, unscrupulous ferry boat operators, and bandits posing as fellow pilgrims. On the other hand, monasteries and hospices were built along the route, offering pilgrims a warm meal and a straw mattress (though they usually had to share the mattress with up to a dozen other pilgrims!).

Whether one was a nobleperson traveling with a retinue of servants or a serf freed at the end of life to make the journey, a pilgrimage was a once-in-a-lifetime experience—oftentimes the last-of-a-lifetime. Thousands died along the pilgrimage routes; one German bishop lost almost half of his 7,000 copilgrims on a trip he organized, and the Crusades began in part because a group of 12,000 Germans was attacked by Bedouins after they left Caesarea in 1065.

Life in the Middle Ages has been famously described as "dull, nasty, brutish, and short." A pilgrimage to a far-off land was an unspeakable and exotic adventure to a person who might otherwise never journey more than 50 kilometers from home. In our world of easy travel, it's difficult to imagine both the trials of the pilgrim's journey and the exultation at reaching the holy shrine.

Theology

Abram, Moses, Jesus, and Paul traveled as a response to God's leading. But, as Paul and Peter make clear in several places, all Christians are "resident aliens." We are citizens of heaven, put on earth to "run the race to completion." This side of Eden, we're all wandering, trying to find our way back to that perfect place where the relationship with God is perfectly intimate. Some have sought to live out this symbolic reality: the early Irish monks wandered because they considered it a way to follow Jesus' example, much like the eighteenth century Russian we met in chapter 5 on the Jesus Prayer.

But pilgrimage isn't aimless wandering. Pilgrimage has a purpose and a goal. Pilgrimage has a destination. Primeval religions before Christianity, Judaism included, held certain spots to be sacred, and the believer was blessed to be in proximity to that sacredness; "the underlying notion was that the sacred consecrates its immediate environment: hence the need to share the environment, the need for an unmediated contact with the sacred." The altar or table that holds the elements of communion has this kind of allure for Christians, as does a pilgrimage to see the relics of a saint. And just as we touch and taste the bread and wine at the

Lord's Supper, a pilgrim endeavors to make physical contact with the remains of a holy person, or with a piece of the cross or a piece of the manger.

Not surprisingly, Christians in the Middle Ages were more open to the supernatural than we are today. Stories abound about miraculous healings that resulted from contact with a relic, for these bones, like the saint to whom they once belonged, were believed to have special powers. While we might think this a holdover from pre-Christian pagan superstition, it was a doctrine officially sanctioned by the church. And when the person in need of healing was unable to make the journey, a family member could make it vicariously for her.

Another reason to make a pilgrimage was for forgiveness of sin, the arduous journey serving as penance either for one big sin or for a lifetime of iniquity. Others made the journey to fulfill a vow made at the time of ordination or in a moment of mortal danger — "Lord, if you get me out of this, I'll go to Santiago!"

And the more holy the saint, the more powerful was his or her shrine. Obviously, being the site of Jesus' Passion, Jerusalem was preeminent. Rome held the remains of Peter and Paul, but it took second place. James, being in the "inner circle" of disciples with Peter and John, made Santiago third. And the list went on from there.

But even if the theology of relics seems dubious today, another reason exists to make a pilgrimage: the journey itself. The medieval pilgrim was walking (at some predetermined places, crawling) for between six months and three years. Without the benefit of a Discman or an mp3 player, there was little to do but talk to your copilgrims, think, or pray. This "peripatetic meditation" had a purifying effect on the pilgrim, and pilgrims returned to their home villages changed. Not only could they tell stories of adventures and ornate cathedrals, they had been reflecting on the state of their lives for weeks on end. This kind of time alone cannot but influence how a person lives out his days.

Robert Brancatelli has studied pilgrimage and has taken dozens of young Christians on pilgrimages. He sees three steps in the journey. The first is *separation*, the time of leaving home and that which is comfortable and familiar. The next stage is the *liminal* period, when the pilgrim is at the edge, the border, the frontier of spirituality — this is when the pilgrim leaves home behind and makes Christ her guide. Finally, *reintegration* into the community takes place, but the former pilgrim is now, in many ways, an adult with an individuated faith of his own.

Brancatelli points to the story of the Prodigal Son in Luke 15:11-32 as an example of this journey. The son separates (v. 11-16), experiences liminality (v. 17-20a), and is ultimately reintegrated into his family (v. 20b-24). "Pilgrimage has the potential to foster conversion in an unprecedented way," writes Brancatelli, "because it allows youth to enter the faith journey on their own terms (physically, emotionally, communally, ideologically)."

practice

Of course, there are all sorts of ways to make a pilgrimage, and all sorts of ways to define pilgrimage. I consider it a mini-pilgrimage every time I drive the two hours to our family's cabin in Minnesota's north woods because I consider the cabin my spiritual home. I also considered it a pilgrimage to fly across the Atlantic and visit Taizé and the Reading Boiler Room. I've also made pilgrimages to the Pine Ridge Indian Reservation in South Dakota and Assisi, Italy, two other places that are spiritually significant to me.

The point is, mental and spiritual preparation and intention are necessary for a pilgrimage to be a pilgrimage. Part of the preparation, especially for American Christians, will be to theologically justify the idea of a pilgrimage. While mission trips to far-off lands are readily accepted by many congregations, a pilgrimage to Jerusalem, Rome, or somewhere else foreign may seem an indulgent waste of money. But while mission trips are wonderful in their own right, pilgrimages serve a different purpose, and they should be planned as such—mission trips, though they shape us inwardly, are primarily about serving others; pilgrimages are an outward expression of an inward journeys.

No doubt, pilgrimages are physically easier now than they have ever been, but there can be some benefit to intentionally creating some challenges along the way. A pilgrim could, as part of the preparation, forego some of the comforts of modern travel—fast food, rolling suitcases, etc. He could choose to prolong the journey by walking or riding a bike for part of the way. In any case, the pilgrim should stay conscious of the purpose of the journey while on the journey. Leaving at home the Discman and *Sports Illustrated* magazine is a first step. Instead, one might take along *The Pilgrim's Progress*, John Bunyan's seventeenth century masterpiece allegory of a Christian's journey from the "City of Destruction" to the "Heavenly City."

Choosing the destination is, obviously, of great importance. Each denomination within the Christian tradition has its own natural pilgrimages. Beyond that, any Christian may become enamored of a certain saint's writings and desire to walk in that person's footsteps. St. Francis of Assisi has had a profound influence on many within the church, and his aura still permeates his hometown in the Umbrian hills of Italy. The Christian community of Northumbria in England has attracted pilgrims recently because of its commitment to communal living and worship; likewise Iona in Scotland. Those who love the writing of Francis Schaefer head to L'Abri; others follow the music to Taizé.

Catholics attend World Youth Day, an official pilgrimage in that tradition; they also visit Lourdes, Fatima, and Guadalupe. Methodists visit Aldersgate, the spot where John Wesley felt his heart "strangely warmed." Presbyterian and Reformed Christians can visit Geneva and see the pulpit from which John Calvin preached his many influential sermons. Congregationalists go to New England to visit the sites made famous by their Pilgrim forebears. Baptists can visit the temple in London where Charles Spurgeon held forth three times per week to massive crowds. Episcopalians and Anglicans follow Chaucer's merry band to Canterbury Cathedral. Lutherans stand before the door in Wittenberg on which Martin Luther posted the *Ninety-Five Theses*. Orthodox Christians travel to Istanbul (formerly Constantinople) to be overwhelmed by the grandeur of the Hagia Sophia. The pilgrimage will gain meaning in the importance of the destination to the pilgrim.

And, of course, the more time that can be taken for the journey, the more impact the trip is likely to have. A weekend sojourn isn't likely to affect the pilgrim as much as a three-month sabbatical pilgrimage to a foreign land. Not everyone can make the time for an extended trip, but the bottom line is, the longer the better. (That is, to a certain point; in the Middle Ages, pilgrimages were sometimes abused when people used them to escape their duties at home!) Indeed, the best pilgrimages may be years in the planning and months in the making. In fact, now might be the time to make a vow to God for a pilgrimage upon your retirement.

A final word

Book V of the *Codex Calixtinus*, the medieval guide for pilgrims to Santiago, gives advice to those who meet pilgrims along the way—advice we can all heed:

> *Pilgrims, whether poor or rich, who return from or proceed to Santiago, must be received charitably and respectfully by all. For he who welcomes them and provides them diligently with lodging will have as his guest not merely the Blessed James, but the Lord himself, who in his gospels said: "He who welcomes you, welcomes me." Many are those who in the past brought upon themselves the wrath of God because they refused to receive the pilgrims of Saint James or the indigent.*

Sunday—Silence, 5 a.m.

This is the best, right now. I'm at the cabin, it's 5 a.m., and everyone else is asleep. We're near the summer solstice, so the days are long. The sun is just coming up over the swamp, there's a little breeze, and all I can hear are leaves, birds, and the coffeemaker. I'll sit on the deck, look at the lake, and let the sun rise up over my back until I hear those little voices in the baby monitor. What will I do during this time? The possibilities are many and thrilling—the Jesus Prayer, Centering Prayer, consolations and desolations, maybe a combination of several. It's so much easier to get out of bed up here, even if I stayed up too late last night. Soli Deo Gloria!

Friday morning, it wasn't so easy to keep silence. I was the only one up here, and it was more lonely than silent when I got up. First thing I turned on NPR for the news and the companionship. But I knew silence was better for me, like broccoli, so I turned off the radio and started to listen. It was good.

chapter fifteen
fasting

Arm yourself manfully against the wickedness of the devil; control the appetite, and you will more easily control all bodily desires.

Thomas à Kempis

I hate fasting.

No, seriously, I *hate* it, and I avoid it at all costs. It is my least favorite of the disciplines in this book. In fact, I wish I didn't have to write about it. I wish it weren't so deeply rooted in the history of God's people. Then I could ignore it.

But I can't ignore it. It's too prevalent, and, honestly, too important. Judged relative to the rest of the world, I am rich. I have an abundance of just about anything I need, especially food. And I really love food. And coffee. I *really* love coffee.

So my experience of fasting has usually been pretty uncomfortable. No. It's been downright horrible. The first meal missed is uncomfortable. The second meal missed is pure agony.

I've never noticed there are *so* many restaurants. And the guy in the car next to me at the stoplight is always eating, usually an enormous caramel roll.

After about 12 hours without food, my headache is nearly unbearable. The lack of calories has conspired with my caffeine addiction to attack my brain. And for some reason, my left shoulder always starts to ache.

I cannot stop thinking about food. I pray, read the Bible, read a novel, try to sleep, and I keep finding myself daydreaming about eating. I'm drinking so much water that I'm in the bathroom about every 30 minutes.

But then, at some point, I turn a corner. Maybe my mind (or spirit) rises above the physical discomfort, or maybe it's because the end is in sight. Usually, I experience some kind of mental and spiritual clarity, some insight, however trivial, about God or myself.

And the break-fast meal is always amazing. Even if it's just beans and rice, every bite is utter bliss, the best thing I've ever tasted. The sense of accomplishment is overwhelming.

But I still hate it.

History

Fasting is a practice common to most religions; it's seen as a sacrifice that gains favor with the Divine, demonstrates self-control, and purifies the body. In the Hebrew Scriptures, there are both public and private fasts, each for different reasons. Public fasts were proclaimed by prophets and monarchs as a sign of national mourning. They were always accompanied by prayer, and often by the wearing of sackcloth and ashes as a sign of penance for sins.

Occasionally, public fasts were called at inauspicious times, like the four days of fasting declared after the fall of Jerusalem, and observed for 70 years. In the midst of a lengthy screed calling Israel back to God, the prophet Joel cries, "Declare a holy fast; call a sacred assembly. Summon the elders and all who live in the land to the house of the Lord your God, and cry out to the Lord."

Other public fasts were normative and connected to holy days. *Yom Kippur*, the Day of Atonement, was the one annual fast day proscribed for the entirety of Israel's existence:

> *This is to be a lasting ordinance for you: On the tenth day of the seventh month you must deny yourselves and not do any work — whether native-born*

or an alien living among you—because on this day atonement will be made for
you, to cleanse you. Then, before the Lord, you will be clean from all your sins.
It is a sabbath of rest, and you must deny yourselves; it is a lasting ordinance.

Here, to "deny yourselves" means to fast from all food and
drink, as well as other bodily gratifications. These annual fasts
were followed by feasts, celebrating the Lord's goodness in granting forgiveness to the people.

Private fasts were held for similar reasons. The psalmist says he
fasted because others whom he loved had become ill, and when
scorned, he fasted until his knees were weak. But, like public
fasts, most individual fasts were done for the sake of penance for
sin, as when David fasted over the fate of his infant child, born to
Bathsheba.

In the New Testament, John the Baptist's followers were
known for their fasting. Jesus continued the biblical exhortations
for fasting, both in his teaching ("But when you fast, put oil on
your head and wash your face, so that it will not be obvious to
men that you are fasting, but only to your Father, who is unseen;
and your Father, who sees what is done in secret, will reward
you"), and in his example ("Then Jesus was led by the Spirit into
the desert to be tempted by the devil. After fasting forty days and
forty nights, he was hungry.").

In the early church, the apostles were known to fast regularly,
and by the time the *Didache* was written around A.D. 60, Chris-
tians were observing every Wednesday and Friday as fast days.
Just as *Yom Kippur* was an annual fast of repentance for the Jews,
Christians observed a repentance fast in the days leading up to
Easter. Although it started as only two days, by the fourth cen-
tury it had expanded to the 40 days we now know as Lent. In the
East, three more periods of fasting were added, including Advent
(the four weeks preceding Christmas), the Fast of the Apostles in
June, and the Fast of the Theotokos (Virgin Mary) in August.

Ancient Christians often followed strict fasting guidelines,
abstaining from all food on fast days. Others refrained only from
meat, eggs, butter, and cheese—these are still the requirements
for many Orthodox Christians. Roman Catholics observe only
Ash Wednesday and Good Friday as official fast days; during
the rest of Lent they are to take only one large meal at midday
and a small meal in the evening. Protestants have generally not
emphasized fasting, even though Luther, Wesley, and Calvin all
commended the practice. Recently, as Protestants have recovered

the rhythms of the liturgical year, fasting during Lent has become more common.

Theology

The Roman Catholic Church teaches, "The Christian fast signifies, above all, an exercise of penitence and sacrifice; but, already for the Fathers, it also had the aim of rendering man more open to the encounter with God and making a Christian more capable of self-dominion and at the same time more attentive to those in need." Indeed, fasting is univocally commended by the Fathers of the early church—along with its partners prayer and silence, it is *the universally applied spiritual discipline:*

Abba John the Dwarf: *"If a king wanted to take possession of his enemies' city, he would begin by cutting off the water and the food and so his enemies, dying of hunger, would submit to him. It is the same with the passions of the flesh: if a man goes about fasting and hungry, the enemies of his soul grow weak."*

Abba Joseph asked Abba Poemen, *"How should one fast?"*

Abba Poemen said to him, *"For my part, I think it is better that one should eat every day, but only a little, so as not to be satisfied."*

Amma Syncletica: *"Just as the most bitter medicine drives out poisonous creatures so prayer joined to fasting drives evil thoughts away."*

Abba Hyperechios: *"Fasting is a check against sin for the monk. He who discards it is like a rampaging stallion."*

St. Gregory of Sinai: *"There are three levels of partaking of food: abstinence, adequacy, and satiety. To abstain means to remain a little hungry after eating; to eat adequately means neither to be hungry nor to be weighed down; to be satiated means to be slightly weighed down. But eating beyond satiety is the door to belly-madness, through which lust comes in. But you, firm in this knowledge, choose what is best for you, according to your powers, without overstepping the limits."*

St. Benedict: *"We believe that two cooked dishes will satisfy the daily needs at each meal—at the sixth and ninth hours…two dishes must be enough for all…. Nothing is more contrary to being a Christian than gluttony."*

Clearly the saints of the church speak with one voice: gluttony is a great sin and fasting is a great virtue. The reason: fasting aids in that great Christian quality, the "mortification of the flesh." Since earliest time—indeed it's a concept set forth powerfully by Jesus and Paul—the appetites or lusts of the body are seen as the root of much evil. Of course, any human being can appreciate the inner battle between the good that the "spirit" wants and the sin that is the tendency of our "flesh."

I use quotation marks around those two because they are separated by a false dichotomy. Neither the Hebrew worldview nor Jesus recognized the body-spirit duality that was made famous by Plato the philosopher and Augustine the theologian. To the contrary, the "mortal coil" which is our physical body, is unified with our soul or spirit. But instead of weakening a theology of fasting, this holistic interpretation actually strengthens it. Physical disciplines aid our spiritual development precisely because the body and the soul are so intricately intertwined.

Thus, one reason we fast is to develop self-control. No concept of personal and corporate spirituality is more central to the Pauline writings than the ideal of self-control. Whether it's with food, sex, words, or even church government, Paul consistently urges moderation and self-control:

Everyone who competes in the games goes into strict training. They do it to get a crown that will not last; but we do it to get a crown that will last forever. Therefore I do not run like a man running aimlessly; I do not fight like a man beating the air. No, I beat my body and make it my slave so that after I have preached to others, I myself will not be disqualified for the prize.

But in a world like ours where, unlike for the saints quoted above, food is known in unparalleled abundance, fasting is now an even more worthy—and difficult—discipline. Two paragraphs from Marjorie Thompson's book, *Soul Feast*, articulate this so clearly they bear repeating in full:

In a more tangible, visceral way than any other spiritual discipline, fasting reveals our excessive attachments and the assumptions that lie behind them. Food is necessary to life, but we have made it more necessary than God. How often have we neglected to remember God's presence when we would never consider neglecting to eat! Fasting brings us face to face with how we put the material world ahead of its spiritual source...

Perhaps we can see, then, that the discipline of fasting has to do with the critical dynamic of accepting those limits which are life-restoring. Our culture would seduce us into believing that we can have it all, do it all, and (even more preposterous!) that we deserve it all. Yet in refusing to accept limits on our consumption or activity, we perpetuate a death-dealing dynamic in the world. That is why the discipline of fasting is so profoundly important today.

Exhibiting self-control and abiding by self-imposed limits are notions antithetical to our consumer-driven culture. The Desert Fathers and Mothers found it so difficult to maintain a life of prayer, silence, and fasting in Jerusalem and other cities that they retreated to the wilderness — and they had never seen a billboard for McDonald's or a TV ad for Mountain Dew! There can be no denying that we live in a world that promotes gluttony and consumption. And the almost weekly news stories and medical reports on "America's Expanding Waistline" corroborate our weakness in this area.

Fasting is a spiritual remedy to what is, really, a spiritual problem. To fast shows our reliance upon God for all things. It reminds us that we are, ultimately, spiritual beings. It confirms that "man does not live by bread alone"; "Everyone who drinks of this water will be thirsty again, but those who drink of the water that I will give them will never be thirsty"; "This is my body which is for you"; and "I am the bread of life."

practice

Fasting from food and drink is the type of fast indicated in Scripture. Richard Foster delineates three types of food-fasts in *Celebration of Discipline*. A "normal fast" is to abstain from all food and drink except water. A "partial fast" is to limit the food intake to significantly less than normal. And an "absolute fast" is to refrain from any eating or drinking. Fasting is known to have health benefits when done correctly, but a spiritual fast obviously has different motivations. Even so, fasting should be done carefully and, when necessary, under the guidance of a physician.

Most individuals find fasting exceedingly difficult because food has both a physical and psychological hold on us. When fasting, one should also moderate one's level of activity — working out, traveling, or not getting enough sleep can lead to sickness or more serious health problems. My experience has been that weakness and muscle soreness is particularly acute upon missing the first and second meals. Beyond that, the feelings of hunger tend to abate somewhat, giving way to spiritual clarity.

But the psychological dependence on food can be even harder to break. Like the college frat boy who feels naked without a beer in his hand at a party, most of our lives are patterned around three meals and many snacks a day, and we feel incomplete without the oral fixation of food (or coffee, or Diet Coke, or chewing gum, and so on). One of the disciplines of the fast is to find other prayerful or otherwise productive ways to use the time usually spent eating and drinking.

For the novice, fasting should be practiced gradually at the beginning. In the week before a fast, smaller meals should be eaten to allow the stomach to shrink. It's beneficial to try several partial fasts before attempting a normal fast. And because the risk of dehydration is high even in a normal fast (we get much of our water in food, so someone on a normal fast should drink lots of water), an absolute fast should be attempted only by someone experienced in fasting.

There are other fasts, too. It can be a powerful practice to participate in either a personal or a communal fast from television. My wife, and I fasted from TV several times until we decided that we would watch no TV in our home every year between Memorial Day and Labor Day. We've also committed ourselves to never having more than one TV in our house. You can imagine the extra time we have to do things like talk, take walks, and write books! Other things to fast from might be trashy magazines, gossip, video games, makeup, or shopping. As with food, any of these can have a stranglehold on our spiritual lives—a stranglehold that can be broken with a fast.

A final word

John Chysostom, the greatest theologian in the Eastern tradition, preached this:

> *Dost thou fast? Give me proof of it by thy works!*
> *Is it said by what kind of works?*
> *If thou seest a poor man, take pity on him!*
> *If thou seest an enemy, be reconciled to him!*
> *If thou seest a friend gaining honor, envy him not!*
> *If thou seest a handsome woman, pass her by!*
> *For let not the mouth only fast, but also the eye, and ear, and the feet, and the hands, and all the members of our bodies.*

Let the hands fast, by being pure from rapine and avarice.

Let the feet fast, but ceasing from running to the unlawful spectacles.

Let the eyes fast, being taught never to fix themselves rudely upon hand-some countenances, or to busy themselves with strange beauties.

For looking is the food of the eyes, but if this be such as is unlawful or forbidden, it mars the fast; and upsets the whole safety of the soul; but if it be lawful and safe, it adorns fasting.

For it would be among things the most absurd to abstain from lawful food because of the fast, but with the eyes to touch even what is forbidden. Dost thou not eat flesh? Feed not upon lasciviousness by means of the eyes.

Let the ear fast also. The fasting of the ear consists in refusing to receive evil speakings and calumnies. "Thou shalt not receive a false report," it says.

Mary Emily Briehl Wells, a high school senior and coauthor of a book of spiritual practices, wrote:

Sometimes Christians fast, refraining from certain or all food and drink for a day or a season…Fasting is a way to say yes to life, together. Ancient communities conserved food during the winter when animals were hibernating and fields lay barren. They restricted their eating so that they could all live until the next harvest. Then they feasted! For Christians, too, fasting is not primarily a solitary discipline any more than feasting is a private event. We fast with others: our Bible study or youth group, our family or congregation. Fasting with others helps focus our attention on the community and God rather than ourselves.

Pilgrimage

    I drove up north this morning. Traffic was light. I put a Byzantine chant on the CD player and watched as all the familiar sites went by—the RV park that used to be packed every weekend is now abandoned; grass has grown up over the signs and the driveway—I wonder if they drained the pool before they left. One barn on the east side of the road finally collapsed last winter, presumably under the weight of snow—no more watching it submit to the forces of gravity every summer. A new subdivision is going up in Princeton—I wonder if they'll be annoyed by the noise from the racetrack.

    I've been reading about the pilgrim's route to Santiago, about all of the sacred stopping points along the way. No relics, per se, on my path. But, nevertheless, these are sights I have known for 34 years—that barn, this gas station, that Dairy Queen. I mark the route and as I journey north, the cares and worries (will I finish painting the trim on the house before the sabbatical ends?) fall away.

chapter sixteen
The sign of the cross and other bodily prayers

If you confide in the Lord, strength will be given you from heaven, and the world and the flesh shall be made subject to you. Neither will you fear your enemy, the devil, if you be armed with faith and signed with the cross of Christ.

Thomas à Kempis

Jay Folley is a Roman Catholic and a friend of mine. He writes:

Every morning there is that heroic moment in which I need to decide between popping out of bed or hitting the snooze button (in which case, the decision will arise again and again every 10 minutes or so). Over the years I have fallen into the habit of signing myself with the cross before I even get out of bed as an intentional way of beginning my day. And I am careful that I sincerely mean to begin the day at that point and not in fact go back to sleep. Because if I decide to reach for my forehead and not the snooze button, the game is on, the day is consecrated to God, and I mean to make the most of it.

As I make the sign of the cross I pray: "God come to my assistance. Lord make haste to help me. Glory be to the Father, and the Son, and the Holy Spirit, as it was in the beginning, is now, and will be forever. Amen."

When I first began this practice, I waited until my feet hit the floor in order to pray; in fact, sometimes I would fall to my knees next to my bed. I loved the very deliberateness of the act, the physical acknowledgment that I need God in order to get through this day. Now however, more often than not, I lie in bed and pray. It may seem that I have gotten lazier, and perhaps I have (to say that I am not a morning person is an understatement), but the intention remains, and in fact, my morning offerings have grown longer and more meaningful. As I lie in the warmth of my bed praying and asking God that I might live according to his will this day, it seems to me more appropriate to be comfortable and secure, as a child would in his father's arms.

This is important to realize: we are body and soul, physical and spiritual, and the prayer and the posture impact each other in profound ways.

There are times when I walk into the chapel at my church and sit cross-legged at the feet of our Lord. Other times I feel I should kneel, and occasionally I will lie face down. Sometimes as I am sitting in the pew, I find myself relaxed, palms open, indicating receptivity; other times I find my head buried in my hands or chest, and I feel that I am searching inwardly.

Your body can tell you a lot about how you are praying. Just recently a person walked into the chapel as I was preparing to deliver a message and caught me pacing up and down the center aisle. I realized I had come to the chapel for peace and inspiration, but had not disposed myself to receive either.

Here then is the secret to all of this—the sign of the cross, kneeling, genuflecting, praying with your hands in the air—these things are not formulas or magic. They do not in themselves produce grace. They are as efficacious as the person is open to receiving the gifts of God. A quick, mindless sign of the cross is as worthless as the Lord's Prayer said in boredom. But a humble and contrite heart coupled with prostrating yourself at the feet of Jesus...oh my...I can only recommend that you try it. It will touch you—body and soul.

History

While Adam, Abraham, and Moses had the distinct pleasure of conversing with God—the Hebrew Scriptures tell us, "The Lord would speak to Moses face to face, as a man speaks with his friend"—more recent followers of God have often felt compelled to use bodily gestures when speaking to the Creator. Biblical prayer postures will be described below in the Theology section, but instead of trying to track the history of multiple gestures, let's look exclusively at one.

The "sign of the cross" is known today as a Catholic and Orthodox practice, having fallen into disrepute among Protestants since the Reformation when it was deemed superstitious. However, this gesture has a long and rich history in the church. Here is a sampling of what some early church fathers wrote about this type of prayer:

> *Tertullian (ca.160-ca.225): "In all our travels and movement, in all our coming in and going out, in putting on of our shoes, at the bath, at the table, in lighting our candles, in lying down, in sitting down, whatever employment occupies us, we mark our foreheads with the sign of the cross."*

> *Hippolytus (ca.170-ca.236): "When tempted, always reverently seal your forehead with the sign of the cross. For this sign of the Passion is displayed and made manifest against the devil if you make it in faith, not in order that you may be seen by men, but by your knowledge putting it forward like a shield."*

> *Cyril of Jerusalem (ca.315-387): "Let us then not be ashamed to confess the Crucified. Be the cross our seal, made with boldness by our fingers on our brow and in every thing; over the bread we eat and the cups we drink, in our comings and in goings; before our sleep, when we lie down and when we awake; when we are traveling, and when we are at rest."*

Early Christians marked themselves with the sign of the cross in several ways: one was to use the thumb to make a small cross on the forehead, the lips, and the chest, thereby asking that God would bless everything thought, spoken, and felt in the heart. Everything in the day was sanctified by this sign, and temptations and evil were thwarted as well. Some evidence suggests that Christians also used this sign surreptitiously to identify one another during times of persecution.

By the middle of the first millennium A.D., Christianity was well known and public throughout the Roman Empire. The sign of the cross developed into a more bold profession, with the right hand touching first the forehead, then the chest, then the right and left shoulders. At some point during the Middle Ages, the Western rite of the Roman Catholic church changed the order to left shoulder-right shoulder, while Byzantine Catholics and Orthodox Christians still make the sign with the right shoulder first.

The position of the fingers also has changed over the years. At first, the small and stealthy sign was made on the forehead using the thumb. The Monophysite controversy of the fifth and sixth centuries introduced a change. The controversy was over the true nature of Jesus Christ: Monophysites argued that Christ had one true nature, but the Council of Chalcedon (451) established that Jesus Christ was one person with two natures (human and divine). In order to physically display their orthodoxy, Christians began to make the sign of the cross with two fingers held together, the index and middle fingers, symbolizing the two natures of Christ.

Later, a tradition developed in the East which also influenced the West where the thumb was held together with the slightly bent index and middle fingers to represent the Trinity and the ring and pinky fingers were bent all the way to the palm to represent the two natures of Christ. While that form is still practiced in the East, Western Christians make the sign of the cross either with the tips of all five fingers held together, representing the five wounds of Christ on the cross, or with the thumb over the bent index finger, forming a cross. In fact, some Roman Catholics kiss their thumb as a sign of reverence to the cross in this lattermost form.

Different verbal prayers have accompanied the sign of the cross over the years. Some of them are:

"The sign of Christ"

"The seal of the living God"

"In the name of Jesus"

"In the name of Jesus of Nazareth"

"In the name of the Holy Trinity"

"Our help is in the name of the Lord"

"O God come to my assistance; O Lord make haste to help me"

"In the name of the Father and of the Son and of the Holy Ghost"
(currently used in the West)

"Holy God, Holy strong One, Holy Immortal One, Have mercy on us"
(currently used in the East).

As this practice of prayer has developed over the centuries, it has taken on new meanings and richness, with even the position of the fingers carrying theological implications. Far from being superstitious, it's a way to engage our bodies in our otherwise cerebral prayers. The *Catechism of the Catholic Church* says of this practice:

> *The sign of the cross…marks with the imprint of Christ the one who is going to belong to him and signifies the grace of the redemption Christ won for us by his cross.*

> *The Christian begins his day, his prayers, and his activities with the sign of the cross: "In the name of the Father and of the Son and of the Holy Spirit. Amen." The baptized person dedicates the day to the glory of God and calls on the Savior's grace which lets him act in the spirit as a child of the Father. The sign of the cross strengthens us in temptations and difficulties.*

Theology

Other physical gestures and postures have been used by people at prayer since biblical times, each one carrying its own theological significance.

Spreading the Palms: This is the most common prayer gesture mentioned in the Bible (e.g., "Then Moses left Pharaoh and went out of the city. He spread out his hands toward the LORD; the thunder and hail stopped, and the rain no longer poured down on the land."). This position is one of petition, in which the pray-er is asking God to fill her hands by granting the request. In early Christian art, the *orant* (Latin for "beg, plead, or pray") was a popular depiction; it's a painting of a figure either kneeling or standing with arms outstretched in prayer, which can be found in the catacombs in Rome and on sarcophagi from the period.

Bending Over, Stooping, Kneeling: The one who delivers the first fruits of the harvest is called upon to bend over as an act of humility before the Lord; the prophet Ezekiel commands everyone who approaches the Temple to bow; the psalmist sings, "Come, let us bow down in worship, let us kneel before the Lord our Maker; for he is our God and we are the people of his pasture, the flock under his care." All these postures are signs of reverence and humility, which remind the pray-er of his subservience to God.

A common practice among Roman Catholics today is *genuflection*, in which the pray-er shows reverence for God and God's holy things by bending down on the right knee. In the Orthodox Church, the similar gesture is *mytania*, a bow from the hips with the legs straight. In both cases the believer signifies bodily that he is repentant, humble, and in need of God's grace—this being the spirit with which a Christian should enter worship.

Prostration: The ultimate sign of humility, to prostrate oneself is to lie face down on the ground. For centuries it was the homage paid by a defeated warrior to the victor in battle; the loser of a battle would lie on the ground and allow the victor to stand on his back. It is a sign of submission, helplessness, and even death. It's also the posture that several people took when they met Jesus:

> *While Jesus was in one of the towns, a man came along who was covered with leprosy. When he saw Jesus, he fell with his face to the ground and begged him, "Lord, if you are willing, you can make me clean." Jesus reached out his hand and touched the man. "I am willing," he said. "Be clean!" And immediately the leprosy left him.*

Other examples of people who fell and prostrated themselves at Jesus' feet are the Syrophoenician woman, Jairus, and Legion. And today, Catholic priests prostrate themselves during their ordination ceremony as a sign of their utter obedience to Christ.

Of course, Christians have prayed in every imaginable posture down through the years, some with more theological heft than others; at our church, we incorporate a new prayer posture every week. The truth on which all these positions rest is that we human beings are body and spirit. We ultimately have one, not two natures. Although Plato and other philosophers divided the flesh from the soul, the Hebrew conception—and the one that Jesus practiced—has always been that humans are unified, body and soul. What we do with our bodies affects our souls, and what we do with our souls affects our bodies.

Therefore, to kneel before God in prayer, whether done privately or in a public worship setting, not only shows God we are humble before him, but it also *does something to us*. And if you really want to have your soul pierced with humility, try prostrating yourself before the Lord in worship.

practice

Kneeling has gotten a bad rap in some circles because it's "required" in some forms of worship. However, if you talk to someone theologically trained in Catholicism, Orthodoxy, or Anglicanism, you will find that in fact it's never required. To kneel after taking the Eucharist in a Catholic mass, for instance, shows reverence for the Lord's Supper. Although many Catholics consider it obligatory, it's meant to be an individual response by the believer.

Similarly, Catholic apologist Al Kresta writes this about genuflection:

Why do Catholics genuflect?

Catholics genuflect because we are in rehearsal for that regenerating moment at the end of history "when every knee shall bow and every tongue confess that Jesus is Lord to the glory of God the Father" (Philippians 2:10-11). We're a little slow at learning, so we thought we'd begin early.

Genuflection is such a small thing. We bend the right knee to the floor and rise up again before a holy person or object. But it's a little gesture that demonstrates some big things: repentance, petition, veneration.

It means that Catholics believe that there is something beyond this material world that we turn to, appeal to, and honor. It means we aren't a law unto ourselves. It means we believe that there is a principle of hierarchy in the universe to which we submit.

In this simple act lies a whole view of God, man, time, eternity, sin, salvation, spirit, and matter. It is a small but submissive response to what God has done in revealing himself to us.

Any Christian would be hard-pressed to disagree with the theology that underlies the act of genuflecting. But, as with any spiritual practice, when the action becomes a meaningless obligation rather than a heartfelt response, something important has been lost. The same could be said of raising hands in some Protestant circles—it has become expected as opposed to sincere. Therefore, the key to practicing a prayer posture is authenticity of spirit.

Ultimately, each of us will find physical postures that best lead us into God's presence. For some it will be standing with hands raised, for others kneeling, and for others sitting with our hands folded or open. Some people will find great meaning in the sign of the cross, while others won't. Since none of these is biblically mandated, it's an open invitation to try them all and discover which is most meaningful for you.

Probably the best thing you can do to challenge yourself is to try praying with postures and gestures that are outside of your own tradition. If you're Catholic, try raising your hands as you sing. If you're Pentecostal, try crossing yourself in the name of the Father, Son, and Holy Spirit whenever you end a prayer.

To visit the worship service of another tradition is most helpful in this regard. Observing and even taking part in the kneeling and sign of the cross in a Catholic worship service, the kissing of an icon in an Orthodox service, or the ecstatic, hands-raised prayer of a Charismatic service will open your eyes to the richness and diversity of the Christian tradition. You can meet with one of the clergy members of that church before or after the service to ask about the meanings behind the movements.

A final word

In his biography of the life of St. Anthony (ca.251-356), St. Athanasius (ca.296-373) quotes Anthony and shows how potent early Christians considered the sign of the cross:

> *Neither ought we to fear the appearances of evil spirits. For they are nothing, but quickly vanish, especially if one defends himself by faith and the sign of the cross.*

Icons

While at Taizé, I decided to purchase an icon. I looked at the many choices there and finally settled on a painting of the Trinity. Actually, it's not a painting but a reproduction of one, on a glossy sort of paper, affixed to a piece of wood. It might be eight inches high and six inches wide.

And now it seems I see and read about that icon everywhere. It turns out it's a reproduction of "The Holy Trinity" by Andrei Rublev, an eighteenth century iconographer. In fact, many people seem to think it's the greatest icon created by the greatest iconographer. Others have said this icon is proof of the existence of God.

It really is a cool icon—the three persons of the Godhead depicted as angels, looking very peaceful. Honestly, I chose that icon because it was so different from all the other "Madonna and Child" icons.

Praying with it has been a new experience for me. I have found contemplating on the icon to be very peaceful, very centering.

chapter seventeen
sabbath

The spiritual person puts the care of his soul before all else.

Thomas à Kempis

During what turned out to be his last year of life, Henri Nouwen was granted a 12-month sabbatical. At the time, he was serving as the chaplain at Daybreak, a community for the developmentally disabled in Toronto. He kept a daily journal that year, which was posthumously published as *Sabbatical Journey: The Diary of His Final Year.* This is from the first entry, dated September 2, 1995:

> *This is the first day of my sabbatical. I am excited and anxious, hopeful and fearful, tired, and full of desire to do a thousand things. The coming year stretches out in front of me as a long, open field full of flowers and full of weeds. How will I cross that field? What will I have learned when I finally reach the other end?*

I feel strange! Very happy and very scared at the same time. I have always dreamt about a whole year without appointments, meetings, lectures, travels, letters, and phone calls, a year completely open to let something radically new happen. But can I do it? Can I let go of all the things that make me feel useful and significant? I realize that I am quite addicted to being busy and experience a bit of withdrawal anxiety. I have to nail myself to a chair and control these wild impulses to get up again and become busy with whatever draws my attention.

But underneath all these anxieties, there is an immense joy. Free at last! Free to think critically, to feel deeply, and to pray as never before. Free to write about the many experiences that I have stored up in my heart and mind during the last nine years. Free to deepen friendships and explore new ways of loving. Free most of all to fight with the Angel of God and ask for a new blessing. The past three months seemed like a steeplechase full of complex hurdles. I have often thought, "How will I ever make it to September?" But now I am here. I have made it, and I rejoice.

The final paragraph of his final entry, Friday, August 30, 1996, reads,

A little later I was back in my own room again. It was full of flowers…There were many balloons and large welcome-home cards with the names and drawings of many community members. What a night! What a warm welcome! Indeed, the sabbatical year is over, and it is good to be back.

History

No commandment is more intricately interwoven in God's covenant with Israel than the edict to keep the Sabbath. It makes its first appearance at the very beginning: when God finished creating the cosmos, he rested on the first-ever Saturday. Dorothy Bass notes that in resting, "God declares as fully possible just how very good creation is. Resting, God takes pleasure in what has been made; God has no regrets, no need to go on to create a still better world or creature more wonderful than the man and woman. In the day of rest, God's free love toward humanity takes form as time shared with them." In other words, God has no need to go on creating, and by ceasing work, God established the six-days-of-work, one-day-of-rest pattern that has guided Judaism ever since.

Sabbath comes from the Hebrew word *shabbat*, which means "to cease." Israel's neighbors knew nothing of a day of rest per

week—the Babylonian calendar only had certain days where
work stopped because the date was deemed evil—so ancient
Israel stood out in its day for having a day dedicated to worship,
prayer, and leisure.

Having escaped the seven-day-per-week drudgery of slavery in
Egypt, God quickly reminded Israel of the importance of keeping
Sabbath. When the manna fell from heaven during the Exodus,
Moses advised the Israelites to gather only enough for one day,
one omer; they quickly found that when they gathered more, it
rotted. However, on the sixth day, Moses told the people to gather two omers worth of manna, since there would be no manna on
the seventh day. Sure enough, some of the more anxious Israelites went out on the seventh morning to collect manna, and there
was none. Upon their return to camp, Moses was scolded by the
Lord, "'How long will you refuse to keep my commandments and
instructions? See! The Lord has given you the Sabbath, therefore
on the sixth day he gives you food for two days; each of you stay
where you are; do not leave your place on the seventh day.' So the
people rested on the seventh day."

Not long after that, God delivered the Ten Commandments to
Moses, the commandment to keep the Sabbath being the longest.
In Exodus, it reads,

> Remember the Sabbath day by keeping it holy. Six days you shall labor and
> do all your work, but the seventh day is a Sabbath to the Lord your God. On
> it you shall not do any work, neither you, nor your son or daughter, nor your
> manservant or maidservant, nor your animals, nor the alien within your gates.
> For in six days the Lord made the heavens and the earth, the sea, and all that is
> in them, but he rested on the seventh day. Therefore the Lord blessed the Sabbath
> day and made it holy.

In this reading, the command to "remember" the Sabbath is
linked to God's creation of the world.

The version in Deuteronomy is somewhat different, for it focuses on the Israelites' release from their nonstop work as slaves:

> Observe the Sabbath day by keeping it holy, as the Lord your God has
> commanded you. Six days you shall labor and do all your work, but the seventh
> day is a Sabbath to the Lord your God. On it you shall not do any work, neither
> you, nor your son or daughter, nor your manservant or maidservant, nor your
> ox, your donkey or any of your animals, nor the alien within your gates, so
> that your manservant and maidservant may rest, as you do. Remember that

you were slaves in Egypt and that the Lord your God brought you out of there
with a mighty hand and an outstretched arm. Therefore the Lord your God has
commanded you to observe the Sabbath day.

Elsewhere in the Torah, details of the Sabbath observance are
recorded: sacrifices may be offered, psalms may be sung, and the
royal guards may be changed, but there was to be no food gather-
ing, plowing or reaping, starting fires, or chopping wood.

And the prophets invoked the fourth commandment more than
any other. Ezekiel equates this commandment to all God's other
commandments; Jeremiah proclaims that the fate of Israel depends
on its ability to keep the Sabbath; and Isaiah exclaims that it's the
primary decree of God, linked to the salvation of the nation:

> *"If you keep your feet from breaking the Sabbath*
> *and from doing as you please on my holy day,*
> *if you call the Sabbath a delight*
> *and the Lord's holy day honorable,*
> *and if you honor it by not going your own way*
> *and not doing as you please or speaking idle words,*
> *then you will find your joy in the LORD,*
> *and I will cause you to ride on the heights of the land*
> *and to feast on the inheritance of your father Jacob."*
> *The mouth of the LORD has spoken.*

With all of this Old Testament material, it's no wonder that
Sabbath keeping was a litmus test by the time Jesus came along.
To the Pharisees' way of thinking, Jesus was lax in his observance of the Sabbath, healing people on the holy day and al-
lowing his disciples to pluck ears of corn. One of the Pharisees'
primary outrages was that Jesus claimed to be "Lord of the Sabbath" and proclaimed, "The Sabbath was made for humankind,
and not humankind for the Sabbath."

Early Christians, especially those of Jewish descent, struggled
to keep the Sabbath, for it seemed like a leftover legalism of rigorous Judaism. Many still observed the Sabbath on Saturday and
celebrated Jesus' resurrection on Sunday. In 321, the Emperor
Constantine decreed Sunday instead of Saturday to be a day of
no work, but of worship of the Lord, thereby effectively changing
the Sabbath to the first day of the week.

In the time since, both Jews and Christians have been guilty of "Sabbatarianism"—that is, excessive strictness in the observance of the Sabbath. Even in Jesus' day, Jewish leaders were doing battle over what it meant to rest from work on the Sabbath. The Jewish Sabbath is observed from sunset Friday through sunset Saturday. Rabbis decided, after reflecting upon God's commands, that 2,000 cubits (just over half a mile) was a "Sabbath day's journey"—walking farther than this would be considered "work". (At the modern excavation of Gezer, stones have been found marking this distance from the walls of the city.)

However, as the people lived with this law, they began to push the rabbis on the definition—what could they get away with legally? You can imagine the conversation:

"Okay, so I can walk 2,000 cubits from my home on the Sabbath."

"Correct."

"Well, if I were to eat a majority of my meals at another place, wouldn't that be considered my home for the day?"

"Hmm, I suppose."

"So, if I were to walk 2,000 cubits on Friday afternoon and eat two meals there on the road, that would be my temporary home for the Sabbath."

"I guess."

"Then, on Saturday morning, I could walk those 2,000 cubits to my temporary home, and then another 2,000 cubits beyond to my friends' home. I will have walked 4,000 cubits without having done any work, technically speaking."

"Technically speaking, I guess you're right."

In fact, that's pretty much what happened. If a person planned it out right, he could get just about anywhere he wanted on the Sabbath and still stay within the law by laying out meals along the way on Friday afternoon. To this day, Orthodox Jews deal with similar issues. Turning on a light switch is considered work in Orthodox Judaism because lighting a fire or lamp was forbidden in the ancient Sabbath laws. One may, however, open the refrigerator on the grounds that any electrical current produced in the process is incidental and without express intention.

However, Sabbatarianism isn't solely the purview of Jews. Three times in the history of the Reformed church, for instance, theologian-politicians have legislated strict Sabbath-keeping laws and heavy punishments for those who break the laws: first in the English and Scottish Reformation of the seventeenth century, then in the Evangelical Revival of the eighteenth century, and again during the Prohibition era of the twentieth century.

Poking around on the Internet, one finds dozens of court cases, editorials and letters to the editor, and elections in which so-called "Blue Laws" are at issue even today. These are the laws that prohibit commerce, especially in alcohol and tobacco, on Sunday. The debate rages that these are legalisms based on a strict Puritan desire to enforce moral behavior on everyone, that it's a church-state separation issue. In any case, one gets the feeling that the battle to force our culture to observe the Sabbath was lost several decades ago.

Theology

Notably, Jesus did not say, "Forget about the Sabbath, it's an old, dead tradition, void of meaning and relevance." No, he said (and his actions indicated) that while the spirit of the law holds, there is a new, higher allegiance—discipleship—that takes precedence.

Now, with the coming of Christ, the Sabbath has taken on new meaning. As well as pointing backward to creation, it points forward to the rest and peace we will have in Christ when he comes again. Thus, early in the church the Sabbath was shifted to Sunday—the day of Jesus' resurrection. And instead of being bound with legalistic obligations, it became known as the "feast day of the Lord." Sunday became a day for Christians to gather for worship, prayer, and a big *agape* meal (love feast), including the Lord's Supper.

Theologian Jürgen Moltmann writes, "If we sum up the commandment and the reason for it, we get the following picture: God creates and shapes a rich and colourful world in order to celebrate the feast of creation with all his creatures on the Sabbath. Therefore the Sabbath is the consummation of creation; without it creation is incomplete and remains insignificant." And as we celebrate it weekly, we have hope in God's final consummation—the return of the Christ!

This, then, is the way of observing the Sabbath that's truest to Scripture: obedience to God's command that we observe the Sabbath day and keep it holy—that we maintain the Sabbath as a day of joyful worship and communion, a day of rest, and a day of reliance upon God. Dorothy Bass writes, "To act as if the world cannot get along without our work for one day in seven is a startling display of pride that denies the sufficiency of our generous maker."

A related concept sheds light on the theological importance of Sabbath. The Law of Moses prescribed that for one out of every seven years, fields were to be given a "Sabbatical Year" to lie fallow. Not only did this preserve the nutrients in the soil and remind the people that the land was not theirs but God's, but it was also commanded that any crops that did grow during the Sabbatical Year were to be left for the poor and the wild animals. So the Sabbatical Year commandment was not only good agricultural policy, it also shaped the ethical identity of Israel as it reminded them to care for the needy in their midst.

practice

Jewish scholars have debated for centuries what should and should not be done on the Sabbath:

> *What should not be done is "work." Defining exactly what that means is a long and continuing argument, but one classic answer is that work is whatever requires changing the natural, material world. All week long, human beings wrestle with the natural world, tilling and hammering and carrying and burning. On the Sabbath, however, Jews let it be. They celebrate it as it is and live in it in peace and gratitude. Humans are created too, after all, and in gratefully receiving the gift of the world, they learn to remember that it is not, finally, human effort that grows the grain and forges the steel. By extension, all activities associated with work or commerce are also prohibited. You are not even supposed to think about them.*

Instead, the Sabbath is to be a day of activities like worship, prayer, family time, lovemaking, naps, and walks.

The thought of trying to practice this in our own lives could hardly seem more countercultural. As our world "speeds up" and people work more, weekends have become the primary time for shopping, mowing the lawn, paying bills, even for holding church committee meetings. And for those of us who work on Sundays, keeping a Sabbath looks even more impossible.

Yet, there's an alternative. I remember hearing a tape by my late friend Mike Yaconelli in which he told pastors to take a full day off. "I take my wife to a motel for the day," Mike said. "We bring a bottle of wine, a couple of novels, and we take the phone off the hook. No one knows where we are. What if a kid shows up at the church in crisis? There are other pastors on the staff who are trained to help people — I figure they can handle it. Then we go home around five and cook a huge meal for our kids."

Keeping a Sabbath isn't a practice that can be achieved slowly, bit by bit, over time. There must be, at some point, a radical break. Decisions must be made by you (and your family) and they must be articulated clearly. Like at Gezer, the boundary stones must be set, never to be moved or walked beyond.

A regular sabbatical is another practice to think about. The majority of this book was written during a three-month sabbatical and I can't overstate the wonderful impact that the time away from work had on my soul. Scour your employee handbook for the sabbatical policy, and if there isn't one, write one up and propose it to your boss.

If you really want to get in trouble with your family and friends, challenge them to keep Sunday as a Sabbath: no soccer games or hockey tournaments, no working at a part-time job, no shopping, no homework. Propose that Sunday be devoted exclusively to things like worship, family brunch, watching the football game, taking a nap, family dinner, and Bible study. Then sit back and watch the fireworks. Watch parents, especially those who know the biblical mandate for Sabbath keeping, try to defend their families' habits and their children's schedules. And watch your children struggle with the way of the world versus the way of Jesus.

Of course, your children could get all their homework done on Friday and Saturday and they could decline to work the Sunday shift, but it will probably be so far from anything they've ever considered that it will take a while for them to regain trust that you are a lucid human being. From there, set up accountability structures and reporting techniques to assist them and you in your practice. And encourage them as they constantly fail in their attempts, because they will fail.

I've talked to so many people over the last several years who have worked to make Sabbath a part of their lives, and their testimony is univocal: it has filled them with joy and peace, love of their friends and family and of God. Sabbath is yet another spiritual practice that at first blush seems to be about giving things up (one day a week to "get things done"), but in the end becomes a gift that is beyond price. In other words, it becomes an addition (of love, joy, hope, peace, etc.) rather than a subtraction.

One reminder, however, is imperative: don't let it become legalistic.

A final word

Jürgen Moltmann writes,

> *The Sabbath opens creation for its true future. On the Sabbath the redemption of the world is celebrated in anticipation. The Sabbath is itself the presence of eternity in time, and a foretaste of the world to come.*

Service

It's day three out in the field in Quiquijana, Peru. Today we spent most of the day building guinea pig pens—one out of wood and five out of adobe bricks—in people's homes. That is, if you can call them homes. One of the places we worked is an adobe structure that might be 10 feet by 10 feet inside. A 90-year-old man lives there, alone. He sleeps on a pile of blankets next to a little fire in which he burns wood and trash. A little walled area adjacent to his home was probably a foot deep with animal dung from wall to wall.

The team that worked on the pen in this home painted a poignant portrait tonight at devotions: almost every one of them, upon seeing the feces they were going to have to wade through as they carried bricks back and forth either thought or said, "You've got to be kidding me." That is, until one of them said, "This is being a servant!" Suddenly their perspective changed and the rest of the day was actually a joy, regardless of the footing.

chapter eighteen
service

Without love, the outward work is of no value; but whatever is done out of love, be it ever so little, is wholly fruitful. For God regards the greatness of love that prompts a man, rather than the greatness of achievement.

Thomas à Kempis

Many of my most profound experiences of union with Christ and with other human beings have taken place in the context of service in Christ's name. On the Pine Ridge and Wind River Indian Reservations, in the Dominican Republic and the mountains of Peru, in the barrios of Juarez, Mexico, and the trailer parks of West Virginia, I've had the great blessing of painting houses, washing the lice out of children's hair, creating a softball field, and building guinea pig pens out of mud bricks. I can genuinely say that each experience has changed me for the better. Each time, the focus of my life has not been me and my needs, but the needs of others. And over time, this cannot help but change my overall perspective in life to be less self-centered and more other-centered.

Aimee, a college student in Kansas City, has had a similar experience:

As an insecure and lonely 15-year-old, I had no real reason to go on the spring break mission trip other than to meet people and feel better about myself. I had few friends and was struggling to find my "place"—that group where I would magically connect, belong, and be loved. Maybe this trip to Juarez, Mexico, would be just the thing I needed to make friends with the kids in my youth group.

Not quite. I felt isolated almost the whole trip; everyone else, it seemed, had their best friends and did not want another. Building houses for impoverished people in Juarez did not even bring the satisfaction I had anticipated.

Something was still missing.

I had chalked the trip up as a loss by the time we had our last group meeting on the night before we were to return. Wrong again. The director of the trip talked to us about John 13 and Jesus' lesson to his disciples about service. Then our leaders did the strangest thing: they lived out Jesus' call to wash one another's feet. Emerging from the kitchen armed with tubs of soapy water and a towel, they proceeded to wash the stinky, sweaty feet of all 35 high school kids. I can only describe what happened when my turn came as a mystical experience. It all suddenly became so clear; the pieces of the gospel message and the experiences of the past few days began to fall into place. I realized in that moment what service is really about: Jesus is real and he loves me.

Six years later, I found myself leading a group of high school students on a similar trip with the same mission organization. This time I had the chance to wash the feet of other people and see the light of recognition go on in their hearts. Jesus' message of service and sacrifice continues to be the most influential, amazing, life-changing thing I have ever encountered.

History

Friends and colleagues who knew I was writing a book on spiritual practices had one overwhelming word of advice: "Please be sure to include a chapter on service." The fear, it seems, is that a book on spiritual disciplines, especially contemplative ones, will encourage navel-gazing—that is, that contemplatives might look inward to the exclusion of serving others.

The history of the church proves otherwise. From the earliest days, the leaders of the church took seriously Jesus' call to serve others. There is, for instance, the famous description of the church in Acts 2:

> *All who believed were together and had all things in common; they would sell their possessions and goods and distribute the proceeds to all, as any had need. Day by day, as they spent much time together in the temple, they broke bread at home and ate their food with glad and generous hearts, praising God and having the goodwill of all the people. And day by day the Lord added to their number those who were being saved.*

Similarly, Acts 4 tells of believers selling their possessions and laying the proceeds at the disciples' feet, and Acts 6 recounts the choosing of seven deacons to look after the needs of widows and others in the community.

Every period of history since has had saints who were not only theologically astute and renowned contemplative pray-ers, but who were also servants:

- The Desert Fathers and Mothers, the archetype contemplatives, never thought that their years in the wilderness were self-serving. Instead, they spent their time praying for the needs of the world—and they also knew that whatever they learned about God in the desert was meant to be shared with everyone.

- In his *Rule*, Benedict of Nursia (480-547) wrote that even cloistered monks are to take in strangers who come to the abbey: "When, therefore, a guest is announced, let him be met by the Superior and the brethren with every mark of charity. And let them first pray together, and then let them associate with one another in peace.... In the greeting let all humility be shown to the guests, whether coming or going; with the head bowed down or the whole body prostrate on the ground, let Christ be adored in them as he is also received."

- In the Middle Ages it was contemplative monks and nuns who cared for and took in persons dying of the Plague, even at the risk of their own lives.

- Francis of Assisi (1182-1226) is famous for shedding his expensive clothes in the town square and covering himself with a burlap sack. He and his fellows took a vow of poverty to show their own humility before the Lord and to be able to work on behalf of the poor with no thought for their own well-being.

- Frederick Bonhoeffer (1906-1945) was ultimately executed for helping Jews to escape the Nazi concentration camps.
- Mother Theresa (1910-1997) became world renowned for her work among the poor and lepers in Calcutta.

In every era, followers of Christ have done their best work when they have looked outward. The best theology is empty without an ethic of service, an ethic that Jesus instituted so explicitly. Thousands of missions, hospitals, and universities have been founded to serve in Jesus' name. Millions of Christians have taken the call to servanthood seriously and stepped out of normalcy and cultural comfort to meet the needs of others. And innumerable billions of acts of kindness take place every year as followers of Christ serve with no intention of seeking recognition or repayment.

Theology

The Bible passages that exhort believers to service in the Lord's name are too numerous to mention, so we will concentrate on one passage:

Then the mother of Zebedee's sons came to Jesus with her sons and, kneeling down, asked a favor of him. "What is it you want?" he asked. She said, "Grant that one of these two sons of mine may sit at your right and the other at your left in your kingdom."

"You don't know what you are asking," Jesus said to them. "Can you drink the cup I am going to drink?"

"We can," they answered. Jesus said to them, "You will indeed drink from my cup, but to sit at my right or left is not for me to grant. These places belong to those for whom they have been prepared by my Father."

When the ten heard about this, they were indignant with the two brothers. Jesus called them together and said, "You know that the rulers of the Gentiles lord it over them, and their high officials exercise authority over them. Not so with you. Instead, whoever wants to become great among you must be your servant, and whoever wants to be first must be your slave—just as the Son of Man did not come to be served, but to serve, and to give his life as a ransom for many."

John Chrysostom (ca.347-407) wrote of this passage, "Do you see how everywhere Jesus encourages them by turning things upside down?" And, indeed, Jesus subverts the common knowledge of our age — and every age — by teaching that the real way to lead is from the position of humble service.

Actually, throughout his earthly ministry, Jesus proves by example time and time again that servanthood is the key to the Kingdom of God about which he's teaching. He preaches that God cares for us so much that he numbers the hairs on our heads; then Jesus exemplifies that divine love by healing a blind man, a leper, and a woman with an issue of blood. In most kingdoms, the rulers act like the Gentiles to whom Jesus refers, but in God's kingdom, the first will be last.

Richard Foster writes that this is "leadership not with a scepter, but with a towel". When Jesus washed his disciples' feet at the Last Supper, he was performing the ultimate act of service to them. Then, after rising, he said to them, "I have set you an example that you should do as I have done for you." There's no wiggle room in that statement, or in the declaration, "Whoever wants to become great among you must be your servant, and whoever wants to be first must be your slave."

Jesus makes no bones about it: his followers serve. Period.

practice

Servanthood is so foundational to the Christian life that it's hard to know where to begin talking about the practice of it. Everything from doing the dishes at home to washing someone's feet to donating one of your kidneys is within the spectrum of service in Jesus' name. For most of us, on most days, Jesus is calling us to tasks somewhere between doing the dishes and donating a kidney — the trick is determining what Jesus is calling me to today.

That's where service intersects with all of the aforementioned practices. For centuries, the Christians who were known for their service to the world were also those Christians who took their spiritual development seriously. When we take time and make space for God to move in our lives, we then have the resources necessary for true servanthood. Ultimately, how you serve Jesus and God's creation is a reflection of your personal spiritual health.

So practice the disciplines and watch yourself become a servant. But let me be quick to say that it's not an "if, then" equation, not a one-way street. Service is good in and of itself. Don't wait to become a contemplative monk to start serving in Christ's name It is part and parcel of following Christ to serve him, for he comes to us in the person of those around us.

A final word

From Richard Foster's *Celebration of Discipline:*

> *More than any other single way, the grace of humility is worked into our lives through the Discipline of service.*

EPILOGUE:
DEVELOPING
A RULE OF LIFE

Service

Today we delivered the guinea pigs to each of the six homes where we built pens! I've seen the inbred cuy that most people in Quiquijana raise and sell (cuy is a great delicacy in Peru) and they are small and sickly. To each home we delivered eight females and one male—and these are some big guinea pigs, like the ones I'm used to seeing at home. Felipe, the World Vision staff person who is responsible for all the farming projects, is then going to follow up with each family and teach them how to breed the cuy when the male is six months old and the females are four months old. The pens keep them separate until they are bred, which is quite different from the normal situation in which the animals freely scurry around the family's living quarters.

I joined the others and we delivered nine cuy to a family in Huarypata. Marcos, the owner of the house, was incredibly proud to receive us into his home, and to show us the new cuy pens. Before we could release the cuy into the pens, he asked us to pray for the cuy, and he asked me to select a verse from his Spanish Bible. I chose Joshua 24:15 "As for me and my household, we will serve the Lord."

To think that our money could buy these cuy, our labor could help construct the pens, and our friends and World Vision could teach the farmers how to breed these animals made a deep impact on our team.

EPILOGUE
DEVELOPING A RULE OF LIFE

*All cannot use the same kind of spiritual exercises,
but one suits this person, and another that. Different
devotions are suited also to the seasons, some being
best for the festivals, and others for ordinary days. We
find some helpful in temptations, others in peace and
quietness. Some things we like to consider when we are
sad, and others when we are full of joy in the Lord.*

Thomas à Kempis

Ultimately, the application of these or any
ancient spiritual practices is up to the individual
Christian, because, while some practices hold
deep meaning for one person, a different set of
practices will appeal to another. And, as Thomas
à Kempis notes in the quote above, different
seasons in our lives call for different disciplines.

However, it's vitally important that each
believer develops a "Rule of Life"—that is, "a
pattern of spiritual disciplines that provides
structure and direction for growth in holiness."

As has been noted often, we live in an era
that's lacking in discipline—in fact, *discipline*

is a dirty word, at least in reference to spirituality. Athletes are encouraged to be disciplined in their diet and workouts, and musicians in their rehearsals, but spiritual discipline is often seen as coercive, if not oppressive.

But on the contrary, spiritual discipline is liberation, for it's within the time set aside to be disciplined that we are changed and shaped by God. The ultimate goal in life for a Christian is that we become *conformed to the image of Christ* and spiritual discipline is the time-tested arena for that change.

Many areas in our life are desperately in need of discipline: sleep, diet, and exercise habits. Self-discipline in any of these areas can (and probably should) be spiritual. Any time you've gone for a run when it was the last thing you wanted to do or passed up a dessert, it has probably tested your spirit! In fact, I received a good word before I wrote my first book: "Writing is a spiritual discipline," my pastor told me. I have found that to be very true. As I write this it's 5 a.m. and it took everything I've got to crawl out of bed and fire up the computer this morning. Writing is indeed a discipline for me, and it's an important part of my Rule.

It may be writing or journaling, it may be exercise or diet; as you examine your life, you may see many areas that need discipline. The best idea is to start with two or three areas of discipline and add to them gradually as you experience some success.

Another way to achieve some success is to orient your Rule around the Christian calendar. Try one discipline during Lent, another during Advent. Use the Lectionary, a three-year daily cycle of Scripture reading, to guide your practice of *lectio divina* or the Daily Office. The church year has certain cycles and patterns that are immensely helpful for the spiritual life.

Following some experience with the ancient practices outlined in this book, you may decide to incorporate some of them into your personal Rule of Life. An example of a rule might look something like this:

- Pray through two centuries of the Jesus Prayer in the morning and evening every day.
- Keep the Sabbath every week from sunset Friday to sunset Saturday.
- Walk a labyrinth once a month.
- Take a two-day silent retreat once a year.
- Fast and walk the Stations of the Cross every Friday during Lent.
- Take a 28-day Ignatian retreat every decade.

You will naturally be more attracted to some practices than others. It is best to start with the ones that are to your liking, but after some time it's good to examine why others are less enticing and then venture into them. Over the span of your life, your Rule will change as you try new practices and move away from others.

In addition to a personal Rule of Life, corporate Rules can be established. We've already looked at the most famous, the *Rule of St. Benedict*. Your family or a group of friends could develop its own Rule, determining the practices that are expected of the group. This might include, for example, daily sacred reading, weekly corporate worship, quarterly service projects, and an annual silent retreat. A team going on a summer church mission trip, for instance, could institute a Rule for the three months of preparation and the week of the trip. Keep in mind that it's best for the group to determine the Rule, rather than have it imposed by a single leader.

Ultimately, my Rule of Life is far more important than most of what I do with my time. Henri Nouwen said, "The spiritual life is not something we add onto an already busy life.... [It] is to impregnate and infiltrate and control what we already do with an attitude of service to God." My Rule is the starting point for ministry—without a Rule, my ministry isn't coming from a deep reservoir of the Holy Spirit but from my own limited human strength.

We have lots of options in our ministries, but developing a disciplined spiritual life isn't one of them. That is, it isn't optional. It's mandatory. And, it's life giving!

Slow down. Listen to God. Be silent. Meditate. Make the Stations. Stare at an icon.

And, there, do you feel it? The divine light of the Risen Christ flickering within you, slowly building to a roaring fire.

The final word

Thomas à Kempis has been our guide throughout this exploration of ancient spiritual practices, and we turn to him one more time for a word of encouragement as we pursue the sacred way:

Strive earnestly for perfection, then, because in a short time you will receive the reward of your labor, and neither fear nor sorrow shall come upon you at the hour of death.

Labor a little now, and soon you shall find great rest, in truth, eternal joy; for if you continue faithful and diligent in doing, God will undoubtedly be faithful and generous in rewarding.

Thomas à Kempis

NOTES

Notes

chapter 1: the quest for god

14 *I fled Him* *The Hound of Heaven*, Francis Thompson (New York: Morehouse, 1988), 4.

22 *Therefore we can with his grace* *Showings*, Julian of Norwich (New York: Paulist, 1978), 186.

chapter 2: what is spirituality and how do you practice it?

26 *Christian spirituality concerns the quest* *Christian Spirituality: An Introduction*, Alister E. McGrath (Malden, Massachusetts: Blackwell, 1999), 2.

  simply the increasing vitality *Soul Feast: An Invitation to the Christian Spiritual Life*, Marjorie J. Thompson, (Louisville: Westminster John Knox, 1995), 6.

  the practice of the presence of God The Practice of the Presence of God, Brother Lawrence (Washington, D.C.: ICS Publications, 1994).

27 *It is a magnificent choreography* Thompson, 6.

  can only be filled *Pensées*, Blaise Pascal (London: Penguin, 1966), 154.

  Get behind me, Satan! Matthew 16:23; Mark 8:33.

29 *Do you not know* 1 Corinthians 9:24-27 (NRSV).

30 *One thing more I have to add.* *Writings from the Philokalia on Prayer of the Heart*, E. Kadloubovsky and G.E.H. Palmer (translators), (London: Faber and Faber, 1951), 92.

  Asceticism reminds us *Amazing Grace: A Vocabulary of Faith*, Kathleen Norris, (New York: Riverhead, 1998), 362, 365.

32 *In the spiritual life* "Moving from Solitude to Community to Ministry," Henri Nouwen, Leadership Journal (Volume XVI, Number 2, Spring 1995), 42.

  Abba Lot went to see Abba Joseph *The Sayings of the Desert Fathers: The Alphabetical Collection*, Benedicta Ward (Kalamazoo: Cistercian, 1975), 88.

chapter 3: silence and solitude

38 *My life is listening* *Thoughts in Solitude*, Thomas Merton (Boston: Shambhala, 1993), 77.

39 *The tongue has the power of life and death* Proverbs 18:21.

  All writers on the spiritual life "Silence," The Catholic Encyclopedia, available at http://www.newadvent.org/cathen/13790a.htm (accessed 13 August, 2004).

  This is the utter desert *The Sayings of the Desert Fathers: The Alphabetical Collection*, Benedicta Ward (Kalamazoo: Cistercian, 1975), 3.

40 *Without silence there is no solitude* *Celebration of Discipline: The Path to Spiritual Growth*, Richard Foster (San Francisco: HarperCollins, 1978), 98.

The seeking out of solitary places   Foster, 97.

41   *Arsenius, flee*   Ward, 8.

The lover of silence   *Ascending the Heights: A Layman's Guide to The Ladder of Divine Ascent*, Fr. John Mack (Ben Lomond, California: Conciliar, 1999), 61.

sound of sheer silence   1 Kings 19:12 (NRSV).

The hermit, all day and all night   *The Monastic Journey*, Thomas Merton (Garden City, New York: Image, 1977), 206-07.

42   *is a joy beyond human comment*   Merton, 210.

Be still, and know that I am God   Psalm 46:10.

Intelligent silence is the mother of prayer   Mack, 60.

the fruit of solitude   Foster, 108.

43   *What interests me most*   *Amazing Grace: A Vocabulary of Faith*, Kathleen Norris (New York: Riverhead, 1998), 17.

44   *As ministers*   *The Way of the Heart*, Henri Nouwen (New York: Ballantine, 1981), 40.

chapter 4: sacred reading

50   *One day I was*   quoted in *Sacred Reading: The Ancient Art of Lectio Divina*, Michael Casey (Ligouri, Missouri: Ligouri Publications, 1995), 59.

51   *It is not a method*   *Amazing Grace: A Vocabulary of Faith*, Kathleen Norris (New York: Riverhead, 1998), 277-278.

52   *I seek you with all my heart*   Psalm 119:10-16.

53   *we need to slow down*   Casey, 83.

54   *From what has been said*   Casey, 62.

55   *Reading is an exterior exercise*   Casey, 60-61.

chapter 5: the jesus prayer

59   *pray without ceasing*   1 Thessalonians 5:17 (NRSV).

pray in the Spirit on all occasions   Ephesians 6:18.

60   *The ceaseless Jesus Prayer*   *The Way of a Pilgrim and The Pilgrim Continues His Way*, Anonymous (Helen Bacovin, translator) (New York: Doubleday, 1978), 20.

Do not waste any time   Anonymous, 22.

63   *To some there comes the spirit of fear*   *Writings from the Philokalia on Prayer of the Heart*, E. Kadloubovsky and G.E.H. Palmer (translators) (London: Faber and Faber, 1951), 83.

Jesus, Moses, and Elijah on the Mount of Transfiguration   Matthew 17:1-8.

Notes

Jesus, son of David, have mercy on me   Mark 10:47 and Luke 18:38.

God, have mercy on me, a sinner   Luke 18:13.

64   *The problem is not in God's willingness to have mercy*   *The Illumined Heart: The Ancient Christian Path of Transformation*, Frederica Mathewes-Green (Brewster, Massachusetts: Paraclete, 2001), 73.

full and perfect knowledge   Kadloubovsky and Palmer, 83.

65   *the mind to descend into the heart*   Kadloubovsky and Palmer, 83.

In ancient times   Mathewes-Green, 63.

66   *When you will be worthy*   Kadloubovsky and Palmer, 270.

chapter 6: centering prayer

68   *there remains a melancholy awareness*   Mathewes-Green, The Illuminated Heart: The Ancient Christian Path of Transformation (Brewster, Massachusetts: Paraclete, 2001), 3.

70   *To maintain an unceasing recollection of God*   Centering Prayer: Renewing an Ancient Christian Prayer Form, M. Basil Pennington, O.C.S.O. (Garden City, New York: Doubleday, 1980), 11-12.

71   *Here is what you are to do*   The Cloud of Unknowing, Anonymous (William Johnston, ed.) (New York: Doubleday, 1973), ch. 3.

Should some thought   Cloud, ch. 7.

God who came to...Elijah in the "sheer silence"   1 Kings 19:12 (NRSV).

73   *Martha is busy...while Mary sits quietly at his feet*   Luke 10:38-42.

forgot all of this   Cloud, ch. 17.

Centering Prayer is an opening   Pennington, 64-65.

The method of Centering Prayer   Pennington, 74.

74   *As you sit comfortably with your eyes closed*   adapted from *http://www.centeringprayer.com/methodcp.htm* (accessed 13 August, 2004).

75   *the fruit of the Spirit: love, joy, peace, patience*   Galatians 5:22-23.

I should think that this kind of prayer   Pennington, 145.

There are some who believe   Cloud, ch. 71.

chapter 7: meditation

77   *The next day John was there again*   John 1:35-39.

81   *on the road to Emmaus*   Luke 24:13-32.

Therefore, one has to interpret correctly   "Some Aspects of Christian Meditation," Congregation for the Doctrine of the Faith, Letter Orationis formas

(15 October, 1989: Acta Apostolicae Sedis 82 [1990], II), available at http://www.cin.org/users/james/fi les/meditation.htm (accessed 13 August, 2004).

Christian meditation can be nothing but Christian Meditation, Hans Urs von Balthasar (San Francisco: Ignatius, 1989), 13.

82 *Contemplative Christian prayer* "Some Aspects of Christian Meditation," 368.

The vistas of God's Word von Balthasar, 27.

84 *When in meditation* von Balthasar, 86.

chapter 8: the ignatian examen

90 *The Exercises come from* "Introduction," in *The Spiritual Exercises of Saint Ignatius*, Pierre Wolff, translator (Liguori, Missouri: Liguori Publications, 1997), ix.

some spiritual exercises by which Wolff, 10.

Deformata reformare adapted from "Spiritual Exercises of St. Ignatius," The Catholic Encyclopedia available at http://www.newadvent.org/cathen/14224b.htm (accessed 13 August, 2004).

Therefore, since we are surrounded Hebrews 12:1-2.

91 *To give thanks to God* adapted from Wolff, 17.

92 *I avoid all thoughts* "Spiritual Exercises", annotation 78-86.

Take, Lord, all my freedom "Spiritual Exercises", annotation 234.

93 *when the soul takes fire* "Spiritual Exercises", annotation 316.

94 *On the contrary* "Spiritual Exercises", annotation 317.

Here I am, O supreme King "Spiritual Exercises", annotation 98.

chapter 9: icons

100 *Perhaps at the foundation* Praying with Icons, Jim Forest (Maryknoll, NewYork: Orbis, 1997), 4.

101 *If we made an image* Forest, 8.

The point about icons Windows into Heaven: The Icons and Spirituality of Russia, Simon Jenkins (Oxford, England: Lion, 1998), 8-9.

103 *The saintliness or the holiness* The Story of Icons, Mary Paloumpis Hallick (Brookline, Massachusetts: Holy Cross Orthodox Press, 2001), 29.

what St. Paul calls a "spiritual body" 1 Corinthians 15:44.

Icons are not easy to "see" Behold the Beauty of the Lord: Praying with Icons, Henri J.M. Nouwen (Notre Dame, Indiana: Ave Maria, 1987), 14.

104 *We do not have to be* Nouwen, 12.

Notes

Previously there was   Christian Spirituality: An Introduction, Alister E. McGrath (Malden, Massachusetts: Blackwell, 1999), 61.

105 Icons…have imprinted themselves   Nouwen, 11-12.

chapter 10: spiritual direction

108 God in the garden "at the time of the evening breeze"   Genesis 3:8 (NRSV).

109 Eli…"realized that the Lord was calling the boy"   1 Samuel 3:8.

the Samaritan woman at the well   John 4:7-30.

He was called "Good Teacher"   Mark 10:17; Luke 18:18.

You must prostrate yourselves   The Lives of the Desert Fathers, Norman Russell and Benedicta Ward (Kalamazoo: Cistercian, 1980), 78.

As far as I am concerned   Holy Listening: The Art of Spiritual Direction, Margaret Guenther (Boston: Cowley, 1992), 52.

110 What happiness, what security, what joy   Guenther, 12.

111 Spiritual direction is not psychotherapy   Guenther, 3.

In my view spiritual direction   'The Best Life:' Eugene Peterson on Pastoral Ministry," David Wood, The Christian Century (Volume 119, Number 6, March 13-20, 2002), 24.

This striving after Christian perfection   "Spiritual Direction," The Catholic Encyclopedia, available at http://www.newadvent.org/cathen/05024a.htm (accessed 13 August, 2004).

112 [T]he sheep listen to his voice.   John 10:3.

113 I have two basic definitions   Wood, 25.

114 A friend is called a guardian   The Way of Friendship, Aelred of Rievaulx (New York: New City Press, 2001), 58.

chapter 11: the daily office

119 Seven times a day I praise you   Psalm 119:164.

going up to the temple   Acts 3:1.

Peter was on a rooftop in Joppa   Acts 10:9.

The apostles used the psalms in their prayers   e.g., Acts 4:23-30.

121 pray without ceasing   1 Thessalonians 5:17 (NRSV).

To accomplish this   The Divine Hours: Prayers for Springtime: A Manual for Prayer, Phyllis Tickle (New York: Doubleday, 2001), ix.

the Divine Hours are prayers of praise   Tickle, x.

122 Keep watch, dear Lord   Venite: A Book of Daily Prayer, Robert Benson (New York: Tarcher/Putnam, 2000), 15.

123 *worship is a "royal 'waste' of time"*   *A Royal 'Waste' of Time: The Splendor of Worshipping God and Being Church for the World*, Marva Dawn (Grand Rapids, Michigan: Eerdmans, 1999).

Asking me why I keep the Offices   *www.thedivinehours.com* (accessed 13 August, 2004).

chapter 12: the labyrinth

129 *Labyrinths are unicursal*   *Walking a Sacred Path: Rediscovering the Labyrinth as a Spiritual Tool* Lauren Artress (New York: Riverhead, 1996, 51.

130 *In 1991, Lauren Artress*   Artress, 1-7.

131 *The labyrinth is an archetype*   "The Labyrinth: Praying Psalm 139," Judy Cannato, *Weavings* (Volume XVIII, Number 3, May/June, 2002, pp. 37-44), 39.

The walk inward becomes a journey   *The Story of Christian Spirituality: Two Thousand Years from East to West*, Gordon Mursell, editor (Minneapolis: Fortress, 2001), 338.

Two truths about labyrinth praying   *Praying the Labyrinth: A Journal for Spiritual Exploration*, Jill Kimberly Hartwell Geffrion (Cleveland, Ohio: Pilgrim, 1999), xiii.

132 *It was during this first walk*   Cannato, 40.

133 *Since the destination is assured*   *Exploring the Labyrinth; A Guide for Spiritual Healing and Growth*, Melissa Gayle West (New York: Broadway, 2000), 5.

chapter 13: stations of the cross

138 *If any want to be my followers*   Matthew 16:24; Mark 8:34; Luke 9:23 (NRSV).

So Pilate decided to grant their demand   Luke 23: 24-28.

139 15 stations adapted from *Meditations and Devotions*, John Henry Cardinal Newman (New York: Longman's and Green, 1893), 155-68.

144 *Dear Jesus, You once were condemned*   *Walk with Jesus: Stations of the Cross*, Henri J.M. Nouwen (Maryknoll, NewYork: Orbis, 1990), 97.

I have set an example that   John 13:15.

147 *The Retreat Master, in one of his conferences*   *The Seven Storey Mountain: An Autobiography of Faith*, Thomas Merton (New York: Harcourt Brace, 1948), 363-364.

chapter 14: pilgrimage

151 *strangers and pilgrims on the earth*   Hebrews 11:13 (NRSV).

152 *it was credited with chasing the devil away*   *The Pilgrim's Guide to Santiago de Compostela*, William Melczer, translator and editor (New York: Ithaca, 1993), 57.

The escarcela had to be narrow and flat   Melczer, 58.

153 *all Christians are "resident aliens"*   e.g., 1 Peter 2:11.

We are citizens of heaven   1 Corinthians 9:24 (NRSV).

the underlying notion   Melczer, 2.

155 *Pilgrimage has the potential to foster conversion*   *Pilgrimage as Rite of Passage: A Guidebook for Youth Ministry*, Robert J. Brancatelli (New York: Paulist, 1998), 55.

157 *Pilgrims, whether poor or rich*   Melczer, 132.

chapter 15: fasting

160 *four days of fasting declared after the fall of Jerusalem*   Zechariah 7:5; 8:19.

Declare a holy fast   Joel 1:14.

This is to be a lasting ordinance for you   Leviticus 16:29-31.

161 *The psalmist…fasted because others…had become ill*   Psalm 35:13-14.

he fasted until his knees were weak   Psalm 109: 24.

David fasted over…his infant child, born to Bathsheba   2 Samuel 12:15-23.

But when you fast, put oil on your head   Matthew 6:17-18.

Then Jesus was led by the Spirit   Matthew 4:1-2.

162 *The Christian fast signifies*   "Some Aspects of Christian Meditation," Congregation for the Doctrine of the Faith, *Letter Orationis formas* (15 October, 1989: *Acta Apostolicae Sedis* 82 [1990], II), available at *http://www.cin.org/users/james/files/meditation.htm* (accessed 13 August, 2004).

Abba John the Dwarf   *The Sayings of the Desert Fathers: The Alphabetical Collection*, Benedicta Ward (Kalamazoo, Michigan: Cistercian, 1975), 74.

Abba Joseph asked Abba Poemen   Ward, 144.

Amma Syncletica   Ward, 193.

Abba Hyperechios   Ward, 200.

St. Gregory of Sinai   *Writings from the Philokalia on Prayer of the Heart*, E. Kadloubovsky and G.E.H. Palmer (translators) (London: Faber and Faber, 1951), 79-80.

St. Benedict   The Rule of St. Benedict, Anthony C. Meisel and M. L. del Mastro (translators) (New York: Doubleday, 1975), 80.

163 *Everyone who competes*   1 Corinthians 9:25-27.

In a more tangible, visceral way   Soul Feast: An Invitation to the Christian Spiritual Life, Marjorie J. Thompson (Louisville, Kentucky: Westminster John Knox, 1995), 71, 74.

164 *man does not live by bread alone*   Matthew 4:4

Everyone who drinks of this water   John 4:13

This is my body which is for you   Corinthians 11:24

I am the bread of life   John 6:48

A "normal fast"   *Celebration of Discipline: The Path to Spiritual Growth*, Richard Foster (San Francisco: HarperCollins, 1978), 49.

165 *Dost thou fast?...*   "The Homilies on the Statutes to the People of Antioch: Homily III," St. John Chrysostom, *Saint Chrysostom on the Priesthood, Ascetic Treatises, Select Homilies and Letters, and Homilies on the Statues: Nicene and Post-Nicene Fathers of the Christian Church, Volume 9* (Peabody, Massachusetts: Hendrickson, 1994), 359.

166 *Sometimes Christians fast*   *Way to Live: Christian Practices for Teens*, Dorothy C. Bass and Don C. Richter (editors) (Nashville: Upper Room, 2002), 73.

chapter 16: the sign of the cross and other bodily prayers

171 *The Lord would speak to Moses*   Exodus 33:11.

Tertullian...Hippolytus...and Cyril of Jerusalem   available at http://www.scborromeo.org/papers/signcros.PDF (accessed 13 August, 2004).

172 *The sign of Christ*   "Sign of the Cross," *The Catholic Encyclopedia*, available at http://www.newadvent.org/cathen/13785a.htm (accessed 13 August, 2004).

173 *The sign of the cross*   *Catechism of the Catholic Church*, available at http://www.christusrex.org/www1/CDHN/baptism.html#CALLED, section1235 (accessed 13 August, 2004).

The Christian begins his day   *Catechism of the Catholic Church*, available at http://www.christusrex.org/www1/CDHN/comm2.html#SECOND, section 2157 (accessed 13 August, 2004).

Then Moses left Pharaoh   Exodus 9:33.

174 *The one who delivers the first fruits*   Deuteronomy 26:10.

Ezekiel commands everyone   Ezekiel 46:3.

Come, let us bow down in worship   Psalm 95:6-7.

While Jesus was in one of the towns   Luke 5:12-13.

The Syrophoenician woman: Mark 7:24-30; *Jairus:* Mark 5:21ff; *Legion:* Luke 8:26-38.

175 *Why do Catholics genuflect?*   *Why Do Catholics Genuflect? And Answers to Other Puzzling Questions About the Catholic Church*, Al Kresta (New York: Chatham House, 2002), 11.

176 *Neither ought we to fear*   *The Life of St. Anthony*, St. Athanasius, section 23, available at http://essenes.net/vita.htm (accessed 13 August, 2004).

chapter 17: sabbath

179 *This is the first day of my sabbatical*   *Sabbatical Journey: The Diary of His Final Year*, Henri J. M. Nouwen (New York: Crossroad, 1998), 3.

180 *A little later I was back*   Nouwen, 222.

God declares as fully possible   "Keeping Sabbath", Dorothy Bass, ed., *Practicing Our Faith: A Way of Life for a Searching People* (San Francisco: Jossey-Bass, 1997), 78.

181 *"How long will you refuse…"*   Exodus 16:28-30 (NRSV).

Remember the Sabbath day   Exodus 20:8-11.

Observe the Sabbath day   Deuteronomy 5:12-15.

182 *If you keep your feet*   Isaiah 58:13-14.

The Sabbath was made for humankind   Mark 2:27 (NRSV).

183 *excavation of Gezer*   *HarperCollins Bible Dictionary*, Paul J. Achtemeier (San Francisco: HarperCollins, 1996), 955.

184 *If we sum up the commandment*   *God in Creation: A New Theology of Creation and the Spirit of God*, Jürgen Moltmann (San Francisco: Harper, 1985), 282.

185 *To act as if the world*   Bass. 86.

Sabbatical Year   Exodus 23; Deuteronomy 15.

crops…to be left for the poor and the wild animals   Exodus 23:10-11.

What should not be done is "work"   Bass, 80.

187 The Sabbath opens creation   Moltmann, 276.

chapter 18: service

191 *All who believed were together*   Acts 2:44-47 (NRSV), emphasis added. [Emphasis didn't show up in the text; waiting to hear back from author which part(s) should be emphasized.]

When, therefore, a guest   *The Rule of St. Benedict*, Anthony C. Meisel and M. L. del Mastro (translators) (New York: Doubleday, 1975), chapter 53.

192 *Then the mother of Zebedee's sons*   Matthew 20:20-28.

193 *Do you see how everywhere*   *Ancient Christian Commentary of Scripture: New Testament 1b: Matthew 14-28*, Manlio Simonetti (editor) (Downers Grove, Illinois: InterVarsity, 2002), 118.

leadership not with a scepter, but with a towel   *Celebration of Discipline: The Path to Spiritual Growth*, Richard Foster (San Francisco: HarperCollins, 1978), 128.

I have set you an example   John 13:15.

whoever wants to become great   Matthew 20:26-27.

194 *More than any other single way*   Foster, 130.

epiloque: peveloping a rule of life

197 *a pattern of spiritual disciplines*   *Soul Feast: An Invitation to the Christian Spiritual Life*, Marjorie J. Thompson (Louisville, Kentucky: Westminster John Knox, 1995), 138.

198 *conformed to the image of Christ*   see Romans 8:29.

199 *The spiritual life is not something we add*   "Deepening Our Conversation with God, Henri Nouwen and Richard Foster, *Leadership Journal* (Volume XVIII, Number 1, Winter 1997), 112.

RESOURCES

Book Resources

Sacred Reading

Boa, Kenneth, *Historic Creeds: A Journal*, Colorado Springs: NavPress, 2000 (117 pp.) and *Sacred Reading: A Journal*, Colorado Springs: NavPress, 2000 (115 pp.). After a good introduction about *lectio*, each book has 90 readings and related questions following the four-part process of reading. This could definitely be used in a youth ministry setting.

Casey, Michael, *Sacred Reading: The Ancient Art of Lectio Divina*, Ligouri, Missouri: Ligouri Publications, 1995 (151 pp.). A Cistercian monk in Australia, Casey sketches the theology and practice of *lectio*, along with a final chapter on reading some traditional texts.

Meisel, Anthony C. and M. L. del Mastro (translators), *The Rule of St. Benedict*, New York: Doubleday, 1975 (117 pp.). As well as the Rule, the translators provide a nice introduction with a history of the monastic movement.

Pennington, M. Basil, O.C.S.O., *Lectio Divina: Renewing the Ancient Practice of Praying the Scriptures*, New York: Crossroad, 1998 (148 pp.). Pennington is on the forefront of the contemplative movement and he provides an excellent understanding of lectio.

Silence and Solitude

Merton, Thomas, *The Silent Life*, New York: Farrar, Strauss, and Giroux, 1957 (178 pp.). Ten years after taking monastic vows, Merton reflected on the silence of the life he had chosen, and the union with Christ that had resulted.

Nouwen, Henri J.M., *The Way of the Heart*, New York: Ballantine, 1981 (81 pp.). This little devotional book has become the modern classic using the Desert Fathers as guides for a modern spirituality.

The Jesus Prayer

Bacovin, Helen (translator), *The Way of a Pilgrim and The Pilgrim Continues His Way*, New York: Doubleday, 1978 (194 pp.). A modern spiritual classic, this work is by an anonymous eighteenth century Russian wayfarer. After a troubled life in which he is injured beyond his capability to work and his young wife dies, the Pilgrim sells all and wanders the Russian countryside attempting to fulfill Jesus' exhortation to "Pray without ceasing." He is told by a spiritual director to use the Jesus Prayer as the basis of his life. This book is very readable, plus it has an appendix with teaching on the Prayer by early church fathers.

Kadloubovsky, E. and G.E.H. Palmer (translators), *Writings from the Philokalia on Prayer of the Heart*, London: Faber and Faber, 1951 (420 pp.). This is a collection from the great writings of the Eastern Fathers that mirrors the selections read by the anonymous author of *The Way of a Pilgrim*.

Mathewes-Green, Frederica, *The Illumined Heart: The Ancient Christian Path of Transformation*, Brewster, Massachusetts: Paraclete, 2001 (112 pp.). An adult convert to Orthodoxy, Mathewes-Green imagines a fifth century Eastern Christian, Anna, and examines the routines of her life to glean lessons for us today. Short and wonderful. She has a nice list of group study questions on her website: www.frederica.com.

Centering Prayer

Anonymous, *The Cloud of Unknowing* (William Johnston, ed.), New York: Doubleday, 1973 (195 pp.). An anonymous fourteenth century treatise on mystical prayer, *The Cloud* is the first mystical classic in English. The author took up the theme of nonintellectual prayer common with many Desert Fathers and applied it as advice from a spiritual father to his disciple.

Keating, Thomas, *Open Mind, Open Heart: The Contemplative Dimension of the Gospel*, New York: Continuum, 2002 (148 pp.). Keating is a Cistercian priest, monk, and abbot who writes a nice history of contemplative prayer in the first chapter and then goes on to teach the principles of Centering Prayer.

Pennington, M. Basil, O.C.S.O., *Centering Prayer: Renewing an Ancient Christian Prayer Form*, Garden City, New York: Doubleday, 1980 (222 pp.). Pennington, a Trappist monk, is a leading authority on Centering Prayer. A retreat leader, speaker, and writer, this is his magnum opus on the Prayer; he has also coauthored the more recent *Centered Living: The Way of Centering Prayer* (Ligouri, Missouri: Ligouri Publications, 1999). Both trace the history of the Prayer, develop it theologically, and give sound and practical advice on its practice.

meditation

Balthasar, Hans Urs von, *Christian Meditation*, San Francisco: Ignatius, 1989 (97 pp.). A short theological treatise on meditation by a giant of twentieth century Catholic theology.

Boyd, Gregory A., *Seeing Is Believing: Experience Jesus through Imaginative Prayer*, Grand Rapids, Michigan: Baker, 2004 (220 pp.). An evangelical pastor, Boyd uses Scripture and tradition to show how imaginative prayer can invigorate an obligation-laden prayer life and even heal hurtful memories.

DeMello, Anthony, *Wellsprings: A Book of Spiritual Exercises*, New York: Doubleday, 1985 (240 pp.). Combining the traditions of the East and the West, DeMello, a Jesuit priest, offers poetry based on Scripture that leads the believer on a journey.

Main, John, *Moment of Christ: The Path of Meditation*, New York: Continuum, 1998 (128 pp.). Benedictine monk John Main combined Christian teaching with Hindu meditation to form a mantra-type meditation. This and other books are compilations of his teachings—he formed communities for meditation in Ealing, England, and Montreal, Canada.

The Ignatian Examen

Ignatius of Loyola, *The Spiritual Exercises of Saint Ignatius* (translated by Pierre Wolff), Liguori, Missouri: Liguori Publications, 1997 (236 pp.). Wolff, a former Jesuit and frequent retreat leader, translates the Exercises into an easily readable American version, and he has helpful notes on each section based on his experience at leading retreats.

Linn, Dennis, Shelia Fabricant Linn, and Matthew Linn, *Sleeping with Bread: Holding What Gives You Life*, Mahwah, New York: Paulist, 1995 (73 pp.). The authors lead Ignatian retreats in hospitals and at retreat centers; they have seen many people deeply affected by ending the day by meditating on that day's consolations and desolations. Francisco Miranda's illustrations give this work the look and feel of a children's book and, indeed, the authors intend to show how simple this practice can be to develop.

icons

Forest, Jim, *Praying with Icons*, Maryknoll, New York: Orbis, 1997 (171 pp.). A friend of Dorothy Day, Henri Nouwen, and Thomas Merton, Jim Forest has traveled in heady theological company. But he left the Catholicism that he shared with those three when he and his wife discovered the potency of prayer with icons. The book shares his journey and what he's learned.

Hallick, Mary Paloumpis, *The Story of Icons*, Brookline, Massachusetts: Holy Cross Orthodox Press, 2001 (80 pp.). A former middle school teacher, Hallick wrote this book for young people. It's easy to read, has some good pictures, and gives examples of important feast days.

Jenkins, Simon, *Windows into Heaven: The Icons and Spirituality of Russia*, Oxford, England: Lion, 1998 (64 pp.). This is like a miniature coffee table book. It gives a nice introduction to the theology and spirituality of icons; then each major feast is introduced with a reflection, an ancient prayer, and a full-page, full-color glossy picture of an icon.

Mathewes-Green, Frederica, *The Open Door: Entering the Sanctuary of Icons and Prayer*, Brewster, Massachusetts: Paraclete, 2003 (144 pp.). This is a beautifully written book which ushers the reader into and through the transcendent and mysterious confines of an Orthodox sanctuary, and, as a result, the history, meaning, and spirituality of icons come alive.

Nouwen, Henri J.M., *Behold the Beauty of the Lord: Praying with Icons*, Notre Dame, Indiana: Ave Maria, 1987 (80 pp.). Collected here are Nouwen's reflections on four different icons, along with fold-out pictures of each icon.

spiritual direction

Aelred of Rievaulx, *The Way of Friendship*, New York: New City Press, 2001 (168 pp.). This spiritual classic lays the groundwork for spiritual friends to listen for the Spirit in one another's lives.

Barry, William A. and William J. Connolly, *The Practice of Spiritual Direction*, San Francisco: HarperCollins, 1981 (209 pp.). Both Barry and Connolly are Jesuit priests who were involved the rebirth of spiritual direction during the 1970s. They trained spiritual directors at the Center for Religious Development in Cambridge, Massachusetts for years, and this book presents their combined wisdom.

Guenther, Margaret, *Holy Listening: The Art of Spiritual Direction*, Boston: Cowley, 1992 (146 pp.). Guenther wrote this modern classic on spiritual direction after years of being an SD, professor, hospital chaplain, and Episcopal priest herself. The SD as spiritual midwife is her guiding metaphor.

Peterson, Eugene, *The Contemplative Pastor: Returning to the Art of Spiritual Direction*, Grand Rapids, Michigan: Eerdmans, 1993 (179 pp.). One of the premier pastors of our time and the translator of The Message, Peterson encourages all pastors to make sacred companionship a hallmark of ministry.

The Daily office

Baillie, John, *A Diary of Private Prayer*, New York: Scribner's, 1949 (130 pp.). These are the morning and evening prayers (one page each) of Baillie, a Scottish chaplain who died in 1960. They cove a month of prayer; this collection has quickly become a devotional classic.

Benson, Robert, *Venite: A Book of Daily Prayer*, New York: Tarcher/Putnam, 2000 (270 pp.). An evangelical convert to the practice of the Office, Benson arranges his book with four Offices per day, including Collects, Psalms, and Gospel readings.

Glenstal Community, *The Glenstal Book of Prayer: A Benedictine Prayer Book*, Collegeville, Minnesota: Liturgical Press, 2001 (150 pp.). This is a wonderful little prayer book that comes from the Benedictine community at Glenstal Abbey in Limerick, Ireland. As well as morning and evening prayers for each day, many of the most famous traditional prayers are recorded herein.

Tickle, Phyllis, *The Divine Hours: Prayers for Autumn and Wintertime: A Manual for*

Prayer, New York: Doubleday, 2000 (651 pp.).

Tickle, Phyllis, *The Divine Hours: Prayers for Springtime: A Manual for Prayer*, New York: Doubleday, 2001 (671 pp.).

Tickle, Phyllis, *The Divine Hours: Prayers for Summertime: A Manual for Prayer*, New York: Doubleday, 2000 (512 pp.). These books are a great gift to the church. In the most readable and accessible fashion imaginable, Tickle has organized and laid out the traditional prayers for morning, noon, and evening, replete with Scripture texts and prayers ancient and modern. Monthly Compline prayers are also included. These books have become my guide for daily prayer.

Webber, Robert (translator and adaptor), *The Prymer: The Prayer Book of the Medieval Era Adapted for Contemporary Use*, Brewster, Massachusetts: Paraclete, 2000 (172 pp.). Webber, the dean of evangelicals who have embraced the pre-Reformation rhythms of church life, has translated the most widely used prayer book of the fifteenth century for twenty-first century use. The book is divided into the eight Daily Offices, but it is also adaptable for a week- or a month-long retreat.

the labyrinth

Artress, Lauren, *Walking a Sacred Path: Rediscovering the Labyrinth as a Spiritual Tool*, New York: Riverhead, 1995 (199 pp.). After an experience at Chartres, Artress went back to her job and started utilizing a labyrinth at Grace Cathedral in San Francisco. The popularity of her project surged and labyrinths have been popping up around North America ever since. This book details her journey.

Hartwell Geffrion, Jill Kimberly, *Praying the Labyrinth: A Journal for Spiritual Exploration*, Cleveland, Ohio: Pilgrim, 1999 (112 pp.), *Living the Labyrinth: 101 Paths to a Deeper Connection with the Sacred*, Cleveland, Ohio: Pilgrim, 2000 (87 pp.), and *Labyrinth and the Song of Songs*, Cleveland, Ohio: Pilgrim, 2003, and *Christian Prayer and Labyrinths: Pathways to Faith, Hope, and Love*. Each of these is a journal that guides you in walking the labyrinth with Scripture and then asks you to journal your thoughts about the journey.

stations of the cross

McKenna, Megan, *The New Stations of the Cross: The Way of the Cross According to Scripture*, New York: Image, 2003 (121 pp.). McKenna focuses on the 15 stations that have been more recently observed by John Paul II, those that are found in the Gospel accounts. She also emphasizes the metaphors of death and suffering along the path.

Nouwen, Henri, *Walk with Jesus: Stations of the Cross*, Maryknoll, New York: Orbis, 1990 (98 pp.). After Nouwen was hit by a car while hitchhiking, he was given drawings of the Stations by Sr. Helen David to reflect on while recuperating in the hospital. The drawings represent the Stations through the suffering and oppression of the world's poor and Nouwen's devotions reflect his many travels to places of poverty.

Whitley, Katerina Katsarka, *Walking the Way of Sorrows: Stations of the Cross*, New York: Morehouse, 1996 (96 pp.). Whitley, in a work of historical fiction, looks at each of the stations through the eyes of an eyewitness.

pilgrimage

Douglas, Deborah and David Douglas, *Pilgrims in the Kingdom: Travels in Christian Britain*, Nashville: Upper Room, 2003 (256 pp.). This beautiful books combines excellent writing and photography to recount the authors' many trips to the British Isles, tracing the rich history of the Christian faith there.

Melczer, William (translator and editor), *The Pilgrim's Guide to Santiago de Compostela*, New York: Ithaca, 1993 (XXX pp.). An academic book, to be sure, but an excellent translation of this medieval text and thus a great companion for anyone making the pilgrimage to Santiago.

Rudolph, Conrad, *Pilgrimage to the End of the World: The Road to Santiago De Compostela*, Chicago: University of Chicago, 2004 (144 pp.). Conrad walked the road to Compostela in 1996, and here he writes about practically everyone one might encounter along the way.

sabbath

Bass, Dorothy, "Keeping Sabbath" in *Practicing Our Faith: A Way of Life for a Searching People* (Dorothy C. Bass, ed.), San Francisco: Jossey Bass, 1997 (232 pp.). Bass's chapter is the best in an all-around excellent book. She uses the history and theology behind the Sabbath to construct a reasonable practice in today's world.

Dawn, Marva, *Keeping the Sabbath Wholly: Ceasing, Resting, Embracing, Healing*, Grand Rapids, Michigan: Eerdmans, 1989 (234 pp.). One of our best practical theologians weighs in on the practice of Sabbath keeping—as always, Dawn is witty and challenging.

Muller, Wayne, *Sabbath: Finding Rest, Renewal, and Delight in Our Busy Lives*, New York: Bantam, 1999 (241 pp.). Muller spells out beautiful and practical ideas that, though rooted in the Judeo-Christian tradition, are applicable to all spiritual people.

---

web Resources (These sites were all accessed on 13 August, 2004)

general sites on spirituality and spiritual practices

www.ccel.org The Christian Classics Ethereal Library, an unparalleled collection of the great writings of the Christian tradition—if it's in the public domain, they've got it.

www.newadvent.org A major Catholic website hosting the entire Catholic Encyclopedia online. *http://www.oca.org/pages/orth_chri/* An index of links and articles on Orthodox Christianity.

sacred Reading

http://www.annarborvineyard.org/tdh/tdh.cfm A church in Ann Arbor, Michigan has the rights to post every day's prayer service on their website, plus it's got lots of great links.

http://www.osb.org/lectio/about.html Links to some of the best primary sources that speak of *lectio* with particular attention to the Benedictine tradition.

The Jesus prayer

http://www.easternchristian.com/prayer-ropes.html Various prayer ropes for reciting the Jesus Prayer are sold here.

http://www.svots.edu/Faculty/Albert-Rossi/Articles/Saying-the-Jesus-Prayer.html A really interesting site on the history and contemporary practice of the Prayer by a member of St. Vladimir's Seminary.

centering prayer

See *www.centeringprayer.com* The Web site of Contemplative Outreach, Ltd., an organization that provides retreats and seminars on centering.

meditation

www.innerexplorations.com This site is "Where Christian mysticism, theology, and metaphysics meet Eastern religions, Jungian psychology and a new sense of the earth." It's got good information defending John Main's style of meditation.
www.christianmeditation.com This is a commercial site that sells tapes and CDs of guided meditation.
www.wccm.org The World Community for Christian Meditation continues the work of John Main from its offices in London. This site hosts bulletin boards, event listings, and books and tapes.

The Ignatian Examen

www.sacredspace.ie The Web site of the Jesuit Communication Centre in Dublin, Ireland. Millions have prayed through a daily Ignatian prayer since this site debuted in 1999. Sacredspace is the gateway for Ignatian prayer in over a dozen languages, and the Kansas City-based ministry organization, YouthFront, has launched *www.sacredgateway.org* using the same content with Flash media technology.

Icons

www.christusrex.org Most of the great Christian artwork of the Western world can be accessed from this fairly unorganized site; e.g., the entirety of the Vatican's collection is here.

spiritual direction

www.sdiworld.org The website of Spiritual Directors International where you can look for an accredited SD in your area.

The Daily office

www.phyllistickle.com The website of the author of The Divine Hours. Information on the books, advice on fixed-hour prayer, and links.
www.praythenews.com A site of Carmelite nuns in Indianapolis that teaches and uses contemplative prayer practices to interact with and pray for the news and needs of the world.
www.taize.fr The Web site for the Taizé community in southern France. Founded by Brother Roger, Taizé is a phenomenon in Europe, attracting thousands of youth and young adults every year. It caters to individuals and groups under 30 years of age. Every day the community gathers three times for singing (they compose all of their own music), prayer, silences, and a Scripture reading. The life of the community revolves around these thrice daily prayer services. The Taizé brothers also lead small groups in the late morning.
www.universalis.com This site is a wonder—it has daily and hourly prayer, the lectionary readings for the day, and links.

Resources

the labyrinth

http://www.veriditas.net/ Spun off from Grace Cathedral (Episcopalian) in San Francisco, Veriditas is the center of the world-wide labyrinth revival. One of their main projects is to collect information on every labyrinth in the world onto an Internet "labyrinth locator."

www.jillkbg.com Jill Geffrion is my personal labyrinth guru and I often walk the labyrinth in her front yard, which you'll see on this site. Her site is full of useful information, links, and resources for purchase.

www.labyrinth.org.uk Virtually walk the labyrinth designed by Jonny Baker and the Youth for Christ London staff.

www.labyrinthsociety.org This site connects most of the people involved in the labyrinth revival and contains many resources.

stations of the cross

http://www.cptryon.org/xpipassio/stations/ Pray the Stations online.

www.robertwilson.com/studio/masterStations.htm Playwright/director/artist Robert Wilson's artistic reflections on the Stations, recently installed at Oberammergau, site of the world-famous Passion Play.

pilgrimage

www.christian-travelers-guides.com Zondervan publishes travel books for many foreign lands with notes on all the important sacred sites in the country. A great resource.

fasting

www.30hourfamine.org Join hundreds of thousands of Christians around the world in February, fasting for 30 hours and raising money for hunger relief.

A short list of christian spiritual classics

Aelred of Rievaulx (twelfth century): *The Way of Friendship* — a reflection on Christ-centered friendships.

Anonymous (fourteenth century): *The Cloud of Unknowing* — a mystical treatise on contemplation; the basis of Centering Prayer.

Anonymous (nineteenth century): *The Way of a Pilgrim* and *The Pilgrim Continues His Way* — a Russian wayfarer discovers the Jesus Prayer during his journeys.

Aquinas, Thomas (thirteenth century): *The Aquinas Prayer Book: The Prayers and Hymns of St. Thomas Aquinas* — one of the greatest theologians of all times at prayer.

Athanasius (fourth century): *The Life of St. Anthony* — the biography of a Desert Father.

Augustine of Hippo (fourth to fifth centuries): *The Confessions* — the greatest spiritual memoir of all time.

Baillie, John (twentieth century): *A Diary of Private Prayer* — 31 daily devotions by a Scottish pastor.

Benedict of Nursia (sixth century): *The Rule of St. Benedict* — the foundation of the Benedictine way of life and spirituality.

Bernard of Clairvaux (twelfth century): *On the Love of God* — a treatise on how to love God and how God loves us.

Bonhoeffer, Dietrich (twentieth century): *The Cost of Discipleship* — a classic on self-sacrifice in Jesus' name.

Bonhoeffer, Dietrich (twentieth century): *Life Together* — his reflection on how Christians need to live in the world and with one another.

Brother Lawrence (seventeenth century): *The Practice of the Presence of God* — the diary of a Carmelite monk who experienced God's presence daily.

Brother Ugolino (thirteenth century): *The Little Flowers of St. Francis* — a biography of the great medieval saint.

Bunyan, John (seventeenth century): *The Pilgrim's Progress* — a metaphor of our journey through the temptations of life.

Catherine of Genoa (fifteenth century): *The Spiritual Dialogue* — a reflection on the soul's purgation and movement toward God.

Catherine of Siena (fourteenth century): *The Dialogue* — the dictation of an ecstatic experience with sections on divine providence, discretion, prayer, obedience.

Chambers, Oswald (nineteenth to twentieth centuries): *My Utmost for His Highest* — a collection of 365 of his devotional writings.

de Sales, Francis (sixteenth to seventeenth centuries): *Introduction to the Devout Life* — a meditation on following Christ in the secular world.

Desert Fathers and Mothers (fourth through nineteenth centuries): *Lives of the Desert Fathers* — a collection of stories of the lives of the desert hermits.

Desert Fathers and Mothers (fourth through nineteenth centuries): *Sayings of the Desert Fathers* — a collection of their sayings on fasting, silence, prayer, and many other categories.

Desert Fathers and Mothers (fourth through nineteenth centuries): *The Philokalia* — a collection of their sayings and writings regarding the Jesus Prayer.

Eckart, Meister (thirteenth or fourteenth centuries): *Collected Works* — a mystical treatise on the intersection between Greek philosophy and Christian theology with an emphasis on God's indwelling of humanity.

Fénelon, François (seventeenth century): *Meditations on the Heart of God* — advice on developing intimacy with God by seeking after his heart.

Fox, George (seventeenth century): The Journal of George Fox — the spiritual memoir of a Quaker leader who was persecuted, yet retained his faith and belief that all humans have access to God.

Hammerskjöld, Dag (twentieth century): *Markings* — journal entries from a Secretary-General of the United Nations who worked for world peace out of his Christian convictions.

Hildegard of Bingen (twelfth century): *Scivias* — description and explanation of 26 mystical visions she received from God, uniting, for the first time, mysticism and doctrine.

Ignatius of Loyola (sixteenth century): *The Spiritual Exercises* — the 28-day retreat during which a believer examines his own life and moves toward unity with Christ.

John Climacus (seventh century): *The Ladder of Divine Ascent* — the handbook for Eastern monastics, it portrays the Christian life as a ladder, each rung a virtue to be mastered.

John of the Cross (sixteenth century): *The Dark Night of the Soul* — an ecstatic poem that traces the soul through its purgation of sin toward union with God in divine love.

Julian of Norwich (fourteenth century): *Showings* — her 16 revelations of God's love, including some beautiful imagery of God as divine Mother.

Kelly, Thomas (twentieth century): *A Testament of Devotion* — five essays by a Quaker teacher about finding the peace of God's presence in the midst of a noisy life.

Resources

Kempis, Thomas à (fifteenth century): *The Imitation of Christ*—possibly the greatest spiritual classic ever written, a mediation on following Christ with humility.

Lewis, C.S. (twentieth century): *Mere Christianity*—a classic on what it means to believe in and follow Christ.

Merton, Thomas (twentieth century): *The Seven Storey Mountain*—the spiritual biography of the twentieth century's most famous monk.

Merton, Thomas (twentieth century): *New Seeds of Contemplation*—Merton's classic treatise on the contemplative life.

Nouwen, Henri J. M. (twentieth century): *In the Name of Jesus*—Nouwen's reflections on the trials and joys of Christian ministry.

Nouwen, Henri J. M. (twentieth century): *The Way of the Heart*—short devotions on the three bases of the contemplative life: solitude, silence, and prayer.

Pascal, Blaise (seventeenth century): *Pensées*—a collection of his notes and essays on science, the weakness of our humanity, and the wager of faith.

Schaeffer, Francis A. (twentieth century): *True Spirituality*—living a life in Christ in the midst of the modern world, focusing on the redemptive power of his resurrection.

Teresa of Ávila (sixteenth century): *The Interior Castle*—her account of building one's soul toward perfection and thus making it a dwelling place for God.

Thérèsa of Lisieux (nineteenth century): *The Story of a Soul*—the autobiography of a mystic who battled illness, died young, and is considered by some to be the great modern saint.

Underhill, Evelyn (twentieth century): *The Spiritual Life*—an outline of the spiritual life and cooperation with God by arguably the greatest mystic of the twentieth century.

Weil, Simone (twentieth century): *Waiting for God*—excerpts of journals, letters, and essays by a convert to Christianity from Judaism who attained almost daily mystical union with Christ.

Woolman, John (eighteenth century): *The Journal of John Woolman*—the spiritual autobiography of a early Quaker who emphasizes revolution through peace and harmony.